F. S. Goodrich.
Albion 1919
Mich.

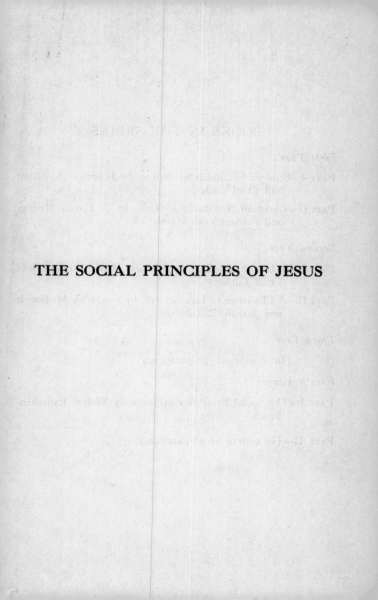

THE SOCIAL PRINCIPLES OF JESUS

BOOKS IN THE SERIES

First Year:

PART I—Student Standards of Action, by Harrison S. Elliott and Ethel Cutler.

PART II—Christian Standards in Life, by J. Lovell Murray and Frederick M. Harris.

Second Year:

PART I—A Life At Its Best, by Richard Henry Edwards and Ethel Cutler.

PART II—A Challenge to Life Service, by Frederick M. Harris and Joseph C. Robbins.

Third Year:

(In course of preparation.)

Fourth Year:

PART I—The Social Principles of Jesus, by Walter Rauschenbusch.

PART II—(In course of preparation.)

COLLEGE   VOLUNTARY   STUDY   COURSES

FOURTH YEAR—PART I

THE SOCIAL
PRINCIPLES OF JESUS

By
WALTER RAUSCHENBUSCH
Professor of Church History, Rochester Theological Seminary

WRITTEN UNDER THE DIRECTION OF
SUB-COMMITTEE ON COLLEGE COURSES
SUNDAY SCHOOL COUNCIL OF EVANGELICAL
DENOMINATIONS
AND
COMMITTEE ON VOLUNTARY STUDY
COUNCIL OF NORTH AMERICAN STUDENT MOVEMENTS

Association Press
NEW YORK: 124 EAST 28TH STREET
LONDON: 47 PATERNOSTER ROW, E.C.
1916

The Bible text printed in short measure (indented both sides) is taken from the American Standard Edition of the Revised Bible, copyright, 1901, by Thomas Nelson & Sons, and is used by permission.

CONTENTS

PART I. THE AXIOMATIC SOCIAL CONVICTIONS OF JESUS

INTRODUCTION vii
I. THE VALUE OF LIFE............................ 1
II. THE SOLIDARITY OF THE HUMAN FAMILY.......... 17
III. STANDING WITH THE PEOPLE..................... 31

PART II. THE SOCIAL IDEAL OF JESUS

IV. THE KINGDOM OF GOD: ITS VALUES.............. 49
V. THE KINGDOM OF GOD: ITS TASKS............... 63
VI. A NEW AGE AND NEW STANDARDS................ 80

PART III. THE RECALCITRANT SOCIAL FORCES

VII. LEADERSHIP FOR SERVICE......................... 97
VIII. PRIVATE PROPERTY AND THE COMMON GOOD........ 116
IX. THE SOCIAL TEST OF RELIGION................... 131

PART IV. CONQUEST BY CONFLICT

X. THE CONFLICT WITH EVIL........................ 151
XI. THE CROSS AS A SOCIAL PRINCIPLE............... 167
XII. A REVIEW AND A CHALLENGE..................... 184

COLLEGE VOLUNTARY STUDY COURSES

"The Social Principles of Jesus" takes seventh place in a series of text-books known as College Voluntary Study Courses. The general outline for this curriculum has been prepared by the Committee on Voluntary Study of the Council of North American Student Movements, representing the Student Young Men's and Young Women's Christian Associations and the Student Volunteer Movement, and the Sub-Committee on College Courses of the Sunday School Council of Evangelical Denominations, representing twenty-nine communions. Therefore the text-books are planned for the use of student classes in the Sunday School, as well as for the supplementary groups on the campus. The present text-book has been written under the direction of these Committees.

The text-books are not suitable for use in the academic curriculum, as they have been definitely planned for voluntary study groups.

This series, covering four years, is designed to form a minimum curriculum for the voluntary study of the Bible, foreign missions, and North American problems. Daily Bible Readings are printed with each text-book. The student viewpoint is given first emphasis—what are the student interests? what are the student problems?

INTRODUCTION

This book is not a life of Christ, nor an exposition of his religious teachings, nor a doctrinal statement about his person and work. It is an attempt to formulate in simple propositions the fundamental convictions of Jesus about the social and ethical relations and duties of men.

Our generation is profoundly troubled by the problems of organized society. The most active interest of serious men and women in the colleges is concentrated on them. We know that we are in deep need of moral light and spiritual inspiration in our gropings. There is an increasing realization, too, that the salvation of society lies in the direction toward which Jesus led. And yet there is no clear understanding of what he stood for. Those who have grown up under Christian teaching can sum up the doctrines of the Church readily, but the principles which we must understand if we are to follow Jesus in the way of life, seem enveloped in a haze. The ordinary man sees clearly only Christ's law of love and the golden rule. This book seeks to bring to a point what we all vaguely know.

It does not undertake to furnish predigested material, or to impose conclusions. It spreads out the most important source passages for personal study, points out the connection between the principles of Jesus and modern social problems, and raises questions for discussion. It was written primarily for voluntary study groups of college seniors, and their intellectual and spiritual needs are not like those of an average church audience. It challenges college men and women to face the social convictions of Jesus and to make their own adjustments.

PART I

THE AXIOMATIC SOCIAL CONVIC-
TIONS OF JESUS

CHAPTER I

THE VALUE OF LIFE

Human Life and Personality are Sacred

Whatever our present conceptions of Jesus Christ may be, we ought to approach our study of his teachings with a sense of reverence. With the slenderest human means at his disposal, within a brief span of time, he raised our understanding of God and of human life to new levels forever, and set forces in motion which revolutionized history.

Of his teachings we have only fragments, but they have an inexhaustible vitality. In this course we are to examine these as our source material in order to discover, if possible, what fundamental ethical principles were in the mind of Jesus. This part of his thought has been less understood and appropriated than other parts, and it is more needed today than ever. Let us go at this study with the sense of handling something great, which may have guiding force for our own lives. Let us work out for ourselves the social meaning of the personality and thought of Jesus Christ, and be prepared to face his challenge to the present social and economic order of which we are part.

How did Jesus view the life and personality of the men about him? How did he see the social relation which binds people together? What was the reaction of his mind in face of the inequalities and sufferings of actual society? If we can get hold of the convictions which were axiomatic and immediate with him on these three questions, we shall have the key to his social principles. We shall take them up in the first three chapters.

DAILY READINGS

FIRST DAY: *The Worth of a Child*

And they were bringing unto him little children, that he should touch them: and the disciples rebuked them. But when Jesus saw it, he was moved with indignation, and said unto them, Suffer the little children to come unto me; forbid them not: for to such belongeth the kingdom of God. Verily I say unto you, Whosoever shall not receive the kingdom of God as a little child, he shall in no wise enter therein. And he took them in his arms, and blessed them, laying his hands upon them.—Mark 10: 13-16.

The child is humanity reduced to its simplest terms. Affectionate joy in children is perhaps the purest expression of social feeling. Jesus was indignant when the disciples thought children were not of sufficient importance to occupy his attention. Compared with the selfish ambition of grownups he felt something heavenly in children, a breath of the Kingdom of God. They are nearer the Kingdom than those whom the world has smudged. To inflict any spiritual injury on one of these little ones seemed to him an inexpressible guilt. See Matthew 18: 1-6.

Can the moral standing of a community be fairly judged by the statistics of child labor and infant mortality? Ignoran

What prompts some young men to tyrannize over their younger brothers? Jealousy Impatience

How does this passage and the principle of the sacredness of life bear on the problem of eugenics?

Rent houses — "no children"

SECOND DAY: *The Humanity of a Leper*

And when he was come down from the mountain, great multitudes followed him. And behold, there came to him a leper, and worshipped him, saying, Lord, if thou wilt, thou canst make me clean. And

he stretched forth his hand, and touched him, saying, I will; be thou made clean. And straightway
his leprosy was cleansed. And Jesus saith unto him,
See thou tell no man; but go, show thyself to the
priest, and offer the gift that Moses commanded, for
a testimony unto them.—Matt. 8: 1-4.

Whenever Jesus healed he rendered a social service to his
fellows. The spontaneous tenderness which he put into his
contact with the sick was an expression of his sense of the
sacredness of life. A leper with fingerless hands and de-
caying joints was repulsive to the æsthetic feelings and a
menace to selfish fear of infection. The community quar-
antined the lepers in waste places by stoning them when they
crossed bounds. (Remember Ben Hur's mother and sister.)
Jesus not only healed this man, but his sense of humanity so
went out to him that "he stretched forth his hand and touched
him." Even the most wretched specimen of humanity still
had value to him.

*What is the social and moral importance of those pro-
fessions which cure or prevent sickness?*

*How would a strong religious sense of the sacredness of
life affect members of these professions?*

THIRD DAY: *The Moral Quality of Contempt*

Ye have heard that it was said to them of old time,
Thou shalt not kill; and whosoever shall kill shall be
in danger of the judgment: but I say unto you, that
every one who is angry with his brother shall be in
danger of the judgment; and whosoever shall say to
his brother, Raca, shall be in danger of the council;
and whosoever shall say, Thou fool, shall be in danger of the hell of fire.—Matt. 5:21, 22.

In the Sermon on the Mount Jesus demanded that the
standards of social morality be raised to a new level. He
proposed that the feeling of anger and hate be treated as

seriously as murder had been treated under the old code, and
if anyone went so far as to use hateful and contemptuous
expressions toward a fellow-man, it ought to be a case for
the supreme court. Of course this was simply a vivid form
of putting it. The important point is that Jesus ranged hate
and contempt under the category of murder. To abuse a man
with words of contempt denies his worth, breaks down his
self-respect, and robs him of the regard of others. It is an
attempt to murder his soul. The horror which Jesus feels
for such action is an expression of his own respect for the
worth of personality.

*How is the self-respect and sense of personal worth of men
built up or broken down in college communities?*
How in industrial communities?

FOURTH DAY: *Bringing Back the Outcast*

Now all the publicans and sinners were drawing
near unto him to hear him. And both the Pharisees
and the scribes murmured, saying, This man receiveth
sinners, and eateth with them.

And he spake unto them this parable, saying, What
man of you, having a hundred sheep, and having lost
one of them, doth not leave the ninety and nine in the
wilderness, and go after that which is lost, until he
find it? And when he hath found it, he layeth it on
his shoulders, rejoicing. And when he cometh home,
he calleth together his friends and his neighbors,
saying unto them, Rejoice with me, for I have found
my sheep which was lost. I say unto you, that even
so there shall be joy in heaven over one sinner that
repenteth, more than over ninety and nine righteous
persons, who need no repentance.

Or what woman having ten pieces of silver, if she
lose one piece, doth not light a lamp, and sweep the
house, and seek diligently until she find it? And
when she hath found it, she calleth together her
friends and neighbors, saying, Rejoice with me, for
I have found the piece which I had lost. Even so,

4

I say unto you, there is joy in the presence of the angels of God over one sinner that repenteth.—Luke 15: 1-10.

Every Jewish community had a fringe of unchurched people, who could not keep up the strict observance of the Law and had given up trying. The pious people, just because they were pious, felt they must cold-shoulder such. Jesus walked across the lines established. What seems to have been the motive that prompted him? Why did the Pharisee withdraw, and why did Jesus mix with the publicans?

What groups in our own communities correspond to the "publicans and sinners," and what is the attitude of religious people toward them?

—*What social groups in college towns are spoken of with contempt by college men, and why?*

—*Is there a Pharisaism of education? Define and locate it.*

FIFTH DAY: *The Problem of the Delinquents*

For the Son of man came to seek and to save that which was lost.—Luke 19: 10.

Here Jesus formulates the inner meaning and mission of his life as he himself felt it. He was here for social restoration and moral salvage. No human being should go to pieces if he could help it. He was not only willing to help people who came to him for help, but he proposed to go after them. The "lost" man was too valuable and sacred to be lost.

How does the Christian impulse of salvation connect with the activities represented in the National Conference of Charities and Correction?

—*How does a college community regard its "sinners"?* Suppose a man has an instinct for low amusements and a yellow sense of honor, how do the higher forces in college life get at that man to set him right?

5

Smokg? Why so many get smokg in college towns?

SIXTH DAY: *Going Beyond Justice*

For the kingdom of heaven is like unto a man that was a householder, who went out early in the morning to hire laborers into his vineyard. And when he had agreed with the laborers for a shilling a day, he sent them into his vineyard. And he went out about the third hour, and saw others standing in the marketplace idle; and to them he said, Go ye also into the vineyard, and whatsoever is right I will give you. And they went their way. Again he went out about the sixth and the ninth hour, and did likewise. And about the eleventh hour he went out and found others standing: and he saith unto them, Why stand ye here all the day idle? They say unto him, Because no man hath hired us. He said unto them, Go ye also into the vineyard. And when even was come, the lord of the vineyard said unto his steward, Call the laborers, and pay them their hire, beginning from the last unto the first. And when they came that were hired about the eleventh hour, they received every man a shilling. And when the first came, they supposed that they would receive more; and they likewise received every man a shilling. And when they received it, they murmured against the householder, saying, These last have spent but one hour, and thou hast made them equal unto us, who have borne the burden of the day and the scorching heat. But he answered and said to one of them, Friend, I do thee no wrong: didst not thou agree with me for a shilling? Take up that which is thine, and go thy way; it is my will to give unto this last, even as unto thee. Is it not lawful for me to do what I will with mine own? or is thine eye evil, because I am good? So the last shall be first, and the first last.—Matt. 20: 1-16.

Judaism rested on legality. So much obedience to the law earned so much reward, according to the contract between God and Israel. Theoretically this was just; practically it gave the inside track to the respectable and welltodo, for it took leisure and money to obey the minutiæ of the Law. In this parable the employer rises from the level of justice to the higher plane of human fellow-feeling. These eleventh-hour men had been ready to work; they had to eat and live; he proposed to give them a living wage because he felt an inner prompting to do so. In the parable of the Prodigal Son the father does more for his son than justice required, because he was a father. Here the employer does more because he is a man. Each acted from a sense of the worth of the human life with which he was dealing. It was the same sense of worth and sacredness in Jesus which prompted him to invent these parables.

Do we find ourselves valuing people according to their utility to us, or do we have an active feeling of their human interest and worth? Let us run over in our minds our family and relatives, our professors and friends, and the people in town who serve us, and see with whom we are on a human footing.

SEVENTH DAY: *The Courtesy of Jesus*

And early in the morning he came again into the temple, and all the people came unto him; and he sat down, and taught them. And the scribes and the Pharisees bring a woman taken in adultery; and having set her in the midst, they say unto him, Teacher, this woman hath been taken in adultery, in the very act. Now in the law Moses commanded us to stone such: what then sayest thou of her? And this they said, trying him that they might have whereof to accuse him. But Jesus stooped down, and with his finger wrote on the ground. But when they continued asking him, he lifted up himself, and said unto them, He that is without sin among you, let him first cast a stone at her. And again he stooped down and with his finger wrote on the ground. And they, when they heard it, went out one by one, beginning from the eldest, even unto the last: and Jesus was left alone, and the woman, where she was, in the midst. And Jesus lifted up himself, and said unto her, Woman,

where are they? did no man condemn thee? And
she said, No man, Lord. And Jesus said, Neither
do I condemn thee: go thy way; from henceforth sin
no more.—John 8: 2-11.

Was there ever a more gentlemanly handling of a raw
situation? This woman was going through one of the most
harrowing experiences conceivable, exposed to the gaze of a
leering and scornful crowd, her good name torn away, her
self-respect crushed. Jesus shielded her from stoning by the
power of his personality and his consummate skill in handling
men. He got inside their guard, aroused their own sense of
past guilt, and so awakened some human fellow-feeling for
the woman. When he was alone with her, what a mingling
of kindness and severity! Surely she would carry away the
memory of a wonderful friend who came to her in her dire
need. Why did Jesus twice turn his eyes away to the ground?
Was he ashamed to look at her shame?

Such a sudden, tragic happening is a severe test of a man's
qualities. It brought out the courtesy of Jesus, his respect for
human personality even in its shame. *How can we train ourselves so that we may be equal to such emergencies?* Would
continued spiritual contact with Jesus be likely to make a
difference?

STUDY FOR THE WEEK

The passages we have studied are inductive material. Can
there be any doubt that Jesus had a spontaneous love for his
fellow-men and a deep sense of the sacredness of human
personality? Physical deformity and moral guilt could not
obscure the divine worth of human life to him. To cause any
soul to stumble and go down, or to express contempt for any
human being, was to him a horrible guilt.

I

This regard for human life was based on the same social

8

instinct which every normal man possesses. But with Jesus it was so strong that it determined all his viewpoints and activities. He affirmed the humane instinct consciously and intelligently, and raised it to the dignity of a social principle. This alone would be enough to mark him out as a new type, prophetic and creative of a new development of the race.

Whence did Jesus derive the strength and purity of his social feeling? Was it simply the endowment of a finely attuned nature? Other fine minds of the ancient world valued men according to their wealth, their rank, their power, their education, their beauty. Jesus valued men as such, apart from any attractive equipment. Why? "The deeper our insight into human destiny becomes, the more sacred does every individual human being seem to us" (Lotze). The respect of Jesus for every concrete person whom he met was due to his religious insight into human life and destiny. But how did he get his insight?

Love and religion have the power of idealistic interpretation. To a mother her child is a wonderful being. To a true lover the girl he loves has sacredness. With Jesus the consciousness of a God of love revealed the beauty of men. The old gods were despotic supermen, mythical duplicates of the human kings and conquerors. The God of Jesus was the great Father who lets his light shine on the just and the unjust, and offers forgiveness and love to all. Jesus lived in the spiritual atmosphere of that faith. Consequently he saw men from that point of view. They were to him children of that God. Even the lowliest was high. The light that shone on him from the face of God shed a splendor on the prosaic ranks of men. In this way religion enriches and illuminates social feeling.

Jesus succeeded in transmitting something of his own sense of the sacredness of life to his followers. As Wundt says: "Humanity in this highest sense was brought into the world by Christianity." The love of men became a social dogma of the Church. Some other convictions of Jesus left few traces on the common thought of Christendom, but the

Church has always stood for a high estimate of the potential worth of the soul of man. It has always taught that man was made in God's image and that he is destined to share in the holiness and eternal life of God.

II

What effects has this registered on social conduct? Has the Church intelligently resisted social forces or conditions which brutalized or shamed men?

It is most difficult to estimate accurately the historic influence of religious ideas. They are subtle and hard to trace. But we can justly reason from our own observations in evangelism and foreign mission work. Those of us who have gone through a clearly marked conversion to Christianity will probably remember that we realized our fellow-men with a new warmth and closeness, and under higher points of view. We were then entering into the Christian valuation of human life. In foreign missions the influence of Christianity can be contrasted with non-Christian social life, and there is often a striking rise in the respect for life and personality as compared with the hardness and callousness of heathen society. This is one of the distinctive marks of the modern and Western world compared with the ancient and the Oriental. Those individuals among us who have really duplicated something of the spirit of Jesus are always marked by their loving regard for human life, even its wreckage. That sense of sacredness is the basis for the whole missionary and philanthropic activity of Christian men and women.

It is also an important force in the social movements. Have there been any widespread, continuous, and successful movements for social justice outside of the territory influenced by Christianity? Was there any causal connection between the historic reformation and purification of Christianity since the sixteenth century and the rise of civil and social democracy? Does the spread of Christian ideas and feelings predispose the powerful classes to make concessions? What contribution did the Wesleyan revival among the working people of England make toward the rise of the trade union movement, the education of stable leaders, and the faith in democracy? It takes idealistic convictions a long time to permeate large social classes, but they often spring into effectiveness suddenly. Certainly a belief in the worth and capacity of the common man is a spiritual support of democratic institutions, and where the Church really spread the Christian sense of the worth and sacredness of human life, it has been a great stabilizer of civil liberty.

Jesus asserted with religious power what all men feel. Sometimes it requires the solemn presence of death to brush aside the artificial distinctions of society and to make us realize that a life is a life, and precious as such. But when we are at our best, we do feel the sacredness of human life.

III

Does our present social order develop or neutralize that feeling in us?

Presumably it works both ways. For those who want to spread the spirit of Christ, it becomes important to inquire at what points our social institutions cheapen life and take the value out of personality.

The class differences inherited from the past are designed to hedge the upper classes about with honor, but they necessarily depreciate the lower classes by contrast and neutralize the tie of the common blood. In some countries the self-respect of the lower classes is affronted by degrading forms of legal punishment reserved for them. Forms of servility are exacted from servants and peasants. The practical working of class differences is most clearly seen in the relation of the sexes. Love is a great equalizer; hence it clashes with class pride. The plot of innumerable dramas and novels turns on the efforts of love to overcome the laws of social caste. Where class spirit is traditional and fully developed, men have a double code for the women of their own class and those of the lower classes. It is a far greater offense for a gentleman to marry a girl of the lower class than to ruin her.

It is the glory of America that our laws do not intend to recognize class differences. The conditions of life on a raw continent and the principles embodied in religious and political idealism fortunately cooperated. Will this last, or are the great differences in wealth once more resulting in definite class lines and in class pride and contempt? What does the phrase "of good family" imply by contrast? What evidence does college fraternity life offer as to the existence of social classes? How is immigration likely to increase the cleavages by adding differences of race and color, religion, language, and manners? What light does the history of immigration in America cast on our valuation of human life in strangers?

Political oligarchies have usually defended their rule by the assumption that the masses are incapable and the few are superior. The laws made by them, however, have usually shown ignorance and indifference as to the human needs of the working masses. The same fundamental adjustment exists in industry. It is not an expression of the worth of the working people if they have no right to organize or to share in governing the conditions under which they work, and if years of good work earn a man no ownership or equity, no legal standing or even tenure of employment in a business. Is the right to petition for a redress of grievances an adequate industrial expression of the Christian doctrine of the worth and sacredness of personality? Is not property essential to the real freedom and self-expression of a human personality?

War and prostitution are the most flagrant offenses against this social principle. War is a wholesale waster of life. Prostitution is the worst form of contempt for personality.

Does our intellectual and scientific work ever tend to chill the warm sense of human values? Do we acquire something of the impassiveness of Nature in studying her enormous waste of life? Do we transfer to human affairs her readiness to use up the masses in order to produce a higher type? Jesus did not talk about eliminating the unfit. He talked about saving them, which requires greater constructive energy if it is really to be done. It also requires a higher faith in the latent recuperative capacities of human nature. The detached attitude of scientific study may combine with our plentiful natural egotism to create a cold indifference toward the less attractive masses of humanity. We need the glow of Christ's feeling for men to come unharmed out of this intellectual temptation.

IV

Doubtless the objection has arisen in our minds that it is not in the interest of the future of the race that religious pity shall coddle and multiply the weak, or put them in control of society.

But did Jesus want the weak to stay weak? Was his social feeling ever maudlin? He was himself a powerful and free personality, who refused to be suppressed or conformed to the dominant type. He challenged the existing authorities, one against the field. Even in the slender record we have of him we can see him running the gamut of emotions from wrath and invective to tenderness and humor. It was precisely his own powerful individuality which made him demand for others the right to become free and strong souls. Other powerful individuals have used up the rest as means to their end. What human life or character did Jesus weaken or break down? He was an emancipator, a creator of strong men. His followers in later times did lay a new yoke on the spirits of men and denied them the right to think their own thoughts and be themselves. But the spirit of Jesus is an awakening force. Even the down-and-out brace up when they come in contact with him, and feel that they are still good for something.

"Jesus Christ was the first to bring the value of every human soul to light, and what he did no one can any more

13

undo" (Harnack). But it remains for every individual to accept and reaffirm that religious faith as his own guiding principle according to which he proposes to live. We shall be at one with the spirit of Christianity and of modern civilization if we approach all men with the expectation of finding beneath commonplace, sordid, or even repulsive externals some qualities of love, loyalty, heroism, aspiration, or repentance, which prove the divine in man. Kant expressed that reverence for personality in his doctrine that we must never treat a man as a means only, but always as an end in himself. So far as our civilization treats men merely as labor force, fit to produce wealth for the few, it is not yet Christian. Any man who treats his fellows in that way, blunts his higher nature; as Fichte says, whoever treats another as a slave, becomes a slave. We might add, whoever treats him as a child of God, becomes a child of God and learns to know God.

"The principle of reverence for personality is the ruling principle in ethics, and in religion; it constitutes, therefore, the truest and highest test of either an individual or a civilization; it has been, even unconsciously, the guiding and determining principle in all human progress; and in its religious interpretation, it is, indeed, the one faith that keeps meaning and value for life" (President Henry C. King).

SUGGESTIONS FOR THOUGHT AND DISCUSSION

I. *The Ordinary Estimate of Men*

1. How much do we care for a man if he is of no practical use to us?

2. On what basis do we ordinarily value men?

II. *Jesus' Estimate of Men*

1. Which source passages in the daily readings seemed to put the feeling of Jesus in the clearest light?

2. How did the religious insight of Jesus reenforce his social feeling?

3. To what extent is it possible to duplicate his sense of humanity without his consciousness of God?

III. *The Valuation of the Individual in Modern Life*

1. List the evidences that modern society values men as such apart from economic utility or standing, or show that it does not so value them.

2. Is the tendency in modern life toward a lower or higher valuation of the individual? To what extent is this due to the influence of Christianity?

3. How do the statistics of industrial accidents agree with our Christian valuation of life?

IV. *The Test of History*

1. What widespread and successful movements for social justice have there been outside the territory influenced by Christianity?

2. How do modern missions serve as an experiment station for the problem of this chapter?

3. What connection was there between the Wesleyan revival and the rise of the trade union movement in England?

V. *For Special Discussion*

1. Do permanent class differences necessarily result in a slighter social feeling for the inferior class?

2. Describe the class lines drawn in your home town.

3. Did you feel these lines more or less when you entered college?

4. Does college life tend to make us callous or sympathetic?

5. Does life in social settlements seem to increase or

decrease respect for human nature in college men and women?

6. How would you preserve your self-respect if you were a working man placed in degrading labor conditions?

7. Does an honor system build up self-respect?

8. Have your scientific studies, and especially evolutionary teachings, increased your regard for humanity in the mass?

9. According to your observation, does religion make a man a stronger or weaker personality?

11-24-19

CHAPTER II

THE SOLIDARITY OF THE HUMAN FAMILY

Men Belong Together

Every man has worth and sacredness as a man. We fixed on that as the simplest and most fundamental social principle of Jesus. The second question is, What relation do men bear to each other?

DAILY READINGS

FIRST DAY: *The Social Impulse and the Law of Christ*

> And one of them, a lawyer, asked him a question, trying him: Teacher, which is the great commandment in the law? And he said unto him, Thou shalt love the Lord thy God with all thy heart, and with all thy soul, and with all thy mind. This is the great and first commandment. And a second like unto it is this, Thou shalt love thy neighbor as thyself. On these two commandments the whole law hangeth, and the prophets.—Matt. 22: 35-40.

Which among the multitudinous prescriptions of the Jewish law ought to take precedence of the rest? It was a fine academic question for church lawyers to discuss. Jesus passed by all ceremonial and ecclesiastical requirements, and put his hand on love as the central law of life, both in religion and ethics. It was a great simplification and spiritualization of religion. But love is the social instinct which binds man and man together and makes them indispensable to one another. Whoever demands love, demands solidarity. Whoever sets love first, sets fellowship high.

When Jesus speaks of love, what more than mere emotion does he mean?

Is love really the highest thing?

What do you think of the epigram of Augustine: Ama et fac quod vis?

Second Day: *Jesus Craving Friendship*

Then cometh Jesus with them unto a place called Gethsemane, and saith unto his disciples, Sit ye here, while I go yonder and pray. And he took with him Peter and the two sons of Zebedee, and began to be sorrowful and sore troubled. Then saith he unto them, My soul is exceeding sorrowful, even unto death: abide ye here, and watch with me. And he went forward a little, and fell on his face, and prayed, saying, My Father, if it be possible, let this cup pass away from me: nevertheless, not as I will, but as thou wilt. And he cometh unto the disciples, and findeth them sleeping, and saith unto Peter, What, could ye not watch with me one hour? Watch and pray, that ye enter not into temptation: the spirit indeed is willing, but the flesh is weak. Again a second time he went away, and prayed, saying, My Father, if this cannot pass away, except I drink it, thy will be done. And he came again and found them sleeping, for their eyes were heavy. And he left them again, and went away, and prayed a third time, saying again the same words. Then cometh he to the disciples, and saith unto them, Sleep on now, and take your rest: behold, the hour is at hand, and the Son of man is betrayed into the hands of sinners. Arise, let us be going: behold, he is at hand that betrayeth me.—Matt. 26: 36-46.

Jesus was personally very sociable. He evidently enjoyed mixing with people. He liked the give-and-take of life. He had friendships. A group of men and women gathered around him who gave him their devoted loyalty. He in turn needed them. The denial of Peter and the betrayal of

Judas hurt him, partly because they were defections from the comradeship of his group. In Gethsemane he craved friendship. He prayed to God, but he reached out for Peter and John. The longing for friendship and the unrest of loneliness are proof of a truly human and social nature.

In how far is a need for others a sign of strength or of weakness?

What connection has the spirit of a team, or the loyalty of a college class, with the Christian law of love?

THIRD DAY: *Restoring Solidarity*

Then came Peter and said to him, Lord, how oft shall my brother sin against me, and I forgive him? until seven times? Jesus saith unto him, I say not unto thee, Until seven times; but, Until seventy times seven.—Matt. 18: 21-22.

Love binds together; hate and anger cut apart. They destroy fellowship. Therefore the chief effort of the Christian spirit must be to reestablish fellowship wherever men have been sundered by ill-will. This is done by confession and forgiveness. Forgiveness was so important to Jesus because social unity was so important to him. In the Lord's Prayer he makes full fellowship with men a condition of full fellowship with God: "Forgive us our debts, as we have forgiven our debtors."

Are there any personal injuries which are beyond forgiveness?

Think back to any striking experience of forgiving or being forgiven. What was the religious and moral reaction on your life?

FOURTH DAY: *The Christian Intensification of Love*

Hereby know we love, because he laid down his life for us: and we ought to lay down our lives for the brethren. But whoso hath the world's goods, and

beholdeth his brother in need, and shutteth up his
compassion from him, how doth the love of God
abide in him? My little children, let us not love in
word, neither with the tongue; but in deed and
truth.—I John 3: 16-18.

Beloved, let us love one another: for love is of
God; and every one that loveth is begotten of God,
and knoweth God. He that loveth not knoweth not
God; for God is love. Herein was the love of God
manifested in us, that God hath sent his only begotten Son into the world that we might live through
him.—I John 4: 7-9.

Beloved, if God so loved us, we also ought to love
one another. No man hath beheld God at any time:
if we love one another, God abideth in us, and his
love is perfected in us.—I John 4: 11-12.

These are quotations from one of the early Christian writings. They are evidence of the emphasis put on love as a
distinctive doctrine of the new religion. Note how the
natural social instinct of human affection is intensified and
uplifted by religious motives and forces. Which of these
motives are directly taken from the personality and life of
Christ?

*Do you remember any quotations from non-Christian litera-
ture in which a similar love for love is expressed?*

FIFTH DAY: *Solidaristic Responsibility*

Then began he to upbraid the cities wherein most
of his mighty works were done, because they repented
not. Woe unto thee, Chorazin! woe unto thee, Beth-
saida! for if the mighty works had been done in
Tyre and Sidon which were done in you, they
would have repented long ago in sackcloth and
ashes. But I say unto you, it shall be more tolerable
for Tyre and Sidon in the day of judgment, than
for you. And thou, Capernaum, shalt thou be exalted

20

unto heaven? thou shalt go down unto Hades: for
if the mighty works had been done in Sodom which
were done in thee, it would have remained until this
day. But I say unto you that it shall be more tolerable for the land of Sodom in the day of judgment,
than for thee.—Matt. 11: 20-24.

We know that by constant common action a social group
develops a common spirit and common standards of action,
which then assimilate and standardize the actions of its
members. Jesus felt the solidarity of the neighborhood
groups in Galilee with whom he mingled. He treated them
as composite personalities, jointly responsible for their moral
decisions.

*What groups of which we have been a part in the past have
stamped us with the group character for good or evil? How
about those of which we are now a part?*

*What have we learned from the Great War about national
solidarity?*

SIXTH DAY: *The Solidarity of the Generations*

Woe unto you, scribes and Pharisees, hypocrites!
for ye build the sepulchres of the prophets, and
garnish the tombs of the righteous, and say, If we had
been in the days of our fathers, we should not have
been partakers with them in the blood of the prophets.
Wherefore ye witness to yourselves, that ye are sons
of them that slew the prophets. Fill ye up then the
measure of your fathers. Ye serpents, ye offspring of
vipers, how shall ye escape the judgment of hell?
Therefore, behold, I send unto you prophets, and wise
men, and scribes: some of them shall ye kill and
crucify; and some of them shall ye scourge in your
synagogues, and persecute from city to city: that
upon you may come all the righteous blood shed on
the earth, from the blood of Abel the righteous unto
the blood of Zachariah son of Barachiah, whom ye
slew between the sanctuary and the altar. Verily I

say unto you, All these things shall come upon this
generation.—Matt. 23: 29-36.

Jesus saw a moral solidarity existing, not only between
contemporaries who act together, but between generations
that act alike. Every generation clings to its profitable wrongs
and tries to silence those who stand for higher righteousness.
Posterity takes comfort in being fairer about the dead issues,
but is just as hot and bad about present issues. The sons
reenact the old tragedies on a new stage, and so line up with
their fathers. In looking back over the history of his nation,
Jesus saw a continuity of wrong which bound the generations together in a solidarity of guilt.

Does the connection consist only in similarity of action,
or is there a causal continuity of wrong in the life of a
community?

*Is there anything in our personal family history or family
wealth and business which threatens to line us up with past
evils?*

SEVENTH DAY: *Social Consciousness in the Lord's Prayer*

After this manner therefore pray ye: Our Father
who art in heaven, Hallowed be thy name. Thy kingdom come. Thy will be done, as in heaven, so on
earth. Give us this day our daily bread. And
forgive us our debts, as we also have forgiven our
debtors. And bring us not into temptation, but
deliver us from the evil one.—Matt. 6: 9-13.

Is there anything more solitary than a human soul calling
to the invisible Presence? Is there anything more social in
consciousness than the Lord's Prayer?

Where in these petitions do you feel the sense of social
coherence as the unspoken presupposition of the thought?[1]

---

[1]Rauschenbusch, "Prayers of the Social Awakening," p. 15, on " The Social
Meaning of the Lord's Prayer."

Could Jesus have thought this prayer if the unity of the race had not been both an instinctive reality and a clear social principle with him?

STUDY FOR THE WEEK

That man is a social being is the fundamental fact with which all social sciences have to deal. We may like or dislike people; we can not well be indifferent to them if they get close to us. As Sartor Resartus puts it: "In vain thou deniest it; thou *art* my brother. Thy very hatred, thy very envy, those foolish lies thou tellest of me in thy splenetic humour; what is all this but an inverted sympathy? Were I a steam-engine, wouldst thou take the trouble to tell lies of me?"

Sex admiration, parental love, "the dear love of comrades," the thrill of patriotism, the joy of play, are all forms of fellowship. They give us happiness because they satisfy our social instinct. To realize our unity gives relish to life. To be thrust out of fellowship is the great pain. Many evil things get their attractiveness mainly through the fact that they create a bit of fellowship—such as it is. The slender thread of good in the saloon is comradeship. (See Jack London, "John Barleycorn.")

I

None ever felt this social unity of our race more deeply than Jesus. To him it was sacred and divine. Hence his emphasis on love and forgiveness. He put his personality behind the natural instinct of social attraction and encouraged it. He swung the great force of religion around to bear on it and drive it home. Anything that substitutes antagonism for fraternity is evil to him. Just as in the case of the natural respect for human life and personality, so in the case of the natural social cohesion of men, he lifted the blind instinct of human nature by the insight of religion and

23

constituted it a fundamental principle of life. It is the business of Christianity to widen the area of comradeship.

Common human judgment assents to the valuation of Jesus. Wherever an effective and stable form of fellowship has been created, a sense of sacredness begins to attach to it, and men defend it as a sort of shrine of the divine in man. Wherever men are striving to create a larger fellowship, they have religious enthusiasm as if they were building a temple for God. This is the heart of church loyalty.

The family is the most striking case of solidarity. It is first formed of two units at opposite poles in point of sex, experience, taste, need, and aims; and when they form it, they usually have as much sense of sacredness as their character is capable of feeling. When children are added, more divergences of age, capacity, and need are injected. Yet out of these contradictory elements a social fellowship is built up, which, in the immense majority of cases, defies the shocks of life and the strain of changing moods and needs, forms the chief source of contentment for the majority of men and women, and, when conspicuously successful, wins the spontaneous tribute of reverence from all right-thinking persons. In using the equipment of the home, in standing by one another in time of sickness and trouble, and in spiritual sympathy, a true family practices solidarity of interests, and furnishes the chief education in cooperation.

Political unity was at first an expansion of family unity. The passionate loyalty with which a nation defends its country and its freedom, is not simply a defence of real estate and livestock, but of its national brotherhood and solidarity. The devotion with which people suffer and die for their State is all the more remarkable because all States hitherto have been largely organizations for coercion and exploitation, and only in part real fraternal communities. Patriotism hitherto has been largely a prophetic outreaching toward a great fellowship nowhere realized. The peoples walk by faith.

What evidence does college life furnish us of the fact that social unity is realized with some sense of sacredness? Why

24

do the years in college stand out in the later memories of graduates with such a glamour? Why do students devote so much unpaid service to their teams and fraternities? Is it for the selfish advantages they hope to get, or because they feel they are realizing the best of life in being part of a solidaristic group? Do the dangers of college organizations prove or disprove the principle that fellowship is felt to be something sacred?

Any historical event in which men stood by their group through suffering or to death is remembered with pride. Any case of desertion or betrayal is remembered with shame. No group forgives those who sell out its solidarity for private safety or profit.

Insurance and cooperation are two great demonstrations of the power of solidarity. In insurance we bear one another's burdens, "and so fulfil the law of Christ." The cooperative associations, which have had such enormous success in Europe, succeed only where neighborhood or common idealistic conviction has previously established a consciousness of social unity. They have to overcome the most adverse conditions in achieving success. When they do, the effect on the economic prosperity of the people and on their moral stability and progressiveness is remarkable.

II

Thus the instincts of the race assent to the social principle of Jesus, that fellowship is sacred. The chief law of Christianity does not contradict the social nature of man but expresses and reenforces it. It is the special function of Christians to promote social unity and expand its blessings. To do this intelligently we should take note where, at present, solidarity is frustrated.

For instance, it is important to inquire how social unity is negatived in commercial life. Is competition necessarily unfraternal? Would a Socialist organization of society necessarily be fraternal? Is it a denial of fellowship to exact monopoly profit from consumers, or to take advantage of the ignorance or necessities of a buyer? Is the law of the market compatible with a fraternal conception of society?

Where can you trace the principle of solidarity actually at work in industrial life? Give cases where you have observed a real sense of human coherence and loyalty between employer and employes. How had the feeling been promoted in those cases and what effect did it have on the economic relations of the two groups? Why is the feeling of antagonism between these groups so common? Does the wages system make this inevitable? How ought we to value the willingness of organized labor to stand together, especially on strike, and what connection does the bitterness toward "scabs" have with our subject?

War is a rupture of fellowship on a large scale. The Great War of 1914 has been the most extensive demonstration of the collapse of love which any of us wants to see. As soon as one nation no longer recognizes its social unity with another nation, all morality collapses, and a deluge of hate, cruelty, and lies follows. The problem of international peace is the problem of expanding the area of love and social unity. It is the sin of Christendom that so few took this problem seriously until we were chastised for our moral stupidity and inertia. The young men and women of today will have to take this problem on their intellect and conscience for their lifetime, and propose to see it through.

III

Does religion create social unity or neutralize it? Does prayer isolate or connect? Has the force of religion in human history done more to divide or to consolidate men?

Evidently religion may work both ways, and all who are interested in it must see to it that their religion does not escape control and wreck fraternity. Even mystic prayer and contemplation, which is commonly regarded as the flower of religious life, may make men indifferent to their fellows.

26

It is worth noting that the prayer experiences of Jesus were not ascetic or unsocial. They prepared him for action. When he went into the desert after his baptism it was to settle the principles on which his Messianic work was to be done; his temptations prove that. When he went out from Capernaum to pray "a great while before day," it was to launch his aggressive missionary campaign among the Galilæan villages. Prayer may be an emotional dissipation. Prayer is Christian only if it makes us realize our fellows more keenly and affectionately.

It is one thing to praise love and another thing to practice it. We may theorize about society and ourselves be contrary and selfish units in it. Social unity is an achievement. A loving mind toward our fellows, even the cranky, is the prize of a lifetime. How can it be evoked and cultivated in us? That is one of the most important problems in education. Can it be solved without religious influences? Love will not up at the bidding. We can observe the fact that personal discipleship of Christ has given some persons in our acquaintance a rare capacity for love, for social sympathy, for peaceableness, for all the society-making qualities. We can make test of the fact for ourselves that every real contact with him gives us an accession of fraternity and greater fitness for nobler social unity. It makes us good fellows.

IV

The man who intelligently realizes the Chinese and the Zulu as his brothers with whom he must share the earth, is an ampler mind—other things being equal—than the man who can think of humanity only in terms of pale-faces. The consciousness of humanity will have to be wrought out just as the consciousness of nationality was gradually acquired. He who has it is ahead of his time and a pioneer of the future. The missionary puts himself in the position to acquire that wider sense of solidarity. By becoming a neighbor to remote people he broadens their conception of humanity and his own, and then can be an interpreter of his new friends to his old friends. The interest in foreign missions has, in fact, been a prime educational force, carrying a world-wide consciousness of solidarity into thousands of plain minds and homes that would otherwise have been provincial in their horizon.

A world-wide civilization must have a common monotheistic faith as its spiritual basis. Such a faith must be unitive and not divisive. What the world needs is a religion with a powerful sense of solidarity.

SUGGESTIONS FOR THOUGHT AND DISCUSSION

I. *Solidarity in Human Life*

1. Are comradeship and team-work instinctive, or must they be learned?

2. Do the symptoms of hatred prove or disprove social unity?

3. Does a strong sense of social unity make a vigorous individualism harder to maintain?

II. *Christianity and Solidarity*

1. Give proof that Jesus felt a human hunger for companionship. *Peter · J. · J – Lazarus – 12*

2. How does the place assigned to love in the teachings of Jesus bear on solidarity? How does the duty of for-giveness connect with this?

3. How does the spirit of the Lord's Prayer prove the place of solidarity in Christianity?

III. *Jesus and the Social Groups*

Q Jerusalem — Mac Capern. Beths – Chor-
1. Where did Jesus treat communities as composite personalities? Would it be equally just today to hold cities responsible as moral units? *Tournany — Jan I.*

2. How did Jesus trace a moral solidarity between generations?

28

IV. *Solidarity in Modern Life*

1. Where do you see the principle of solidarity accepted and where do you see it denied in modern social life?

2. In what way does war outrage Jesus' principles of social unity? Does it ever promote fraternity and solidarity? If so how?

3. Is class consciousness a denial of social solidarity or an approach to it? How can group loyalty be made to contribute to the common weal?

4. How should we value the willingness of organized labor to stand together, particularly on strike? What light does bitterness toward scabs throw on social solidarity?

5. Why is the feeling of antagonism between employer and employe so common? Does a wage system make this inevitable? Can a real sense of cooperation be secured? If so how?

6. If a manufacturer has a monopoly, how much profit will loyalty to Christian principles permit him to make?

7. When is competition unfraternal? Would socialism insure fraternity? *Wht = S? "Bolshevism with a shave Lit. Dig.*

8. Do college fraternities practice fraternity? *Belong to a frat?*

V. *Strengthening Solidarity*

1. How can the law of love be made the basis of modern business?

2. Does religion create social unity or neutralize it? How about prayer?

3. How does the Christian law of love bear on the relations of the races in America?

4. What have Christian missions done to lead society from the nationalistic to the international and inter-racial stage?

5. Can world-wide social unity be secured without the influence of Christianity?

VI. *For Special Discussion*

1. To what extent does our present commercial and

industrial organization furnish a basis for experience of
solidarity and education in it?

2. What aspects of modern advertising are Christian and
which are non-Christian?

3. To what extent is the law of the market compatible
with a fraternal conception of society?

4. Would a successful socialist organization create a
stronger sense of solidarity or would divisive interests get
in by new ways?

5. Which has the better inducements to loyalty, a college, or a trade union? Which has more of it? *Why?*

6. How does the team spirit go wrong among students?

CHAPTER III

STANDING WITH THE PEOPLE

The Strong Must Stand Up for the Weak

We have found two simple and axiomatic social principles in the fundamental convictions of Jesus: The sacredness of life and personality, and the spiritual solidarity of men. Now confront a mind mastered by these convictions with the actual conditions of society, with the contempt for life and the denial of social obligation existing, and how will he react? How will he see the duty of the strong, and his own duty?

DAILY READINGS

FIRST DAY: *The Social Platform of Jesus*

And he came to Nazareth, where he had been brought up: and he entered, as his custom was, into the synagogue on the sabbath day, and stood up to read. And there was delivered unto him the book of the prophet Isaiah. And he opened the book, and found the place where it was written,

The Spirit of the Lord is upon me,
Because he anointed me to preach good tidings to the poor:
He hath sent me to proclaim release to the captives,
And recovering of sight to the blind,
To set at liberty them that are bruised,
To proclaim the acceptable year of the Lord.

And he closed the book, and gave it back to the attendant, and sat down: and the eyes of all in the synagogue were fastened on him. And he began to say unto them, To-day hath this scripture been fulfilled in your ears. And all bare him witness, and

wondered at the words of grace which proceeded out
of his mouth: and they said, Is not this Joseph's
son?—Luke 4: 16-22.

Luke evidently felt that this appearance of Jesus in the
synagogue of his home city at the outset of his public work
was a significant occasion. The passage from Isaiah (61: 1f)
was doubtless one of the favorite quotations of Jesus. He
saw his own aims summarized in it and he now announced
it as his program. Its promises were now about to be realized.
What were they? Glad tidings for the poor, release for the
imprisoned, sight for the blind, freedom for the oppressed,
and a "year of Jehovah." If this was an allusion to the year
of Jubilee (Lev. 25), it involved a revolutionary "shedding
of burdens," such as Solon brought about at Athens. At any
rate, social and religious emancipation are woven together in
these phrases. Plainly Jesus saw his mission in raising to
free and full life those whom life had held down and hurt.

"As thou didst send me into the world, even so sent I
them." Must the platform of Jesus be our platform and
program?

SECOND DAY: *The Social Test of the Messiah*

And the disciples of John told him of all these
things. And John calling unto him two of his disciples sent them to the Lord, saying, Art thou he that
cometh, or look we for another? And when the men
were come unto him, they said, John the Baptist hath
sent us unto thee, saying, Art thou he that cometh,
or look we for another? In that hour he cured many
of diseases and plagues and evil spirits; and on many
that were blind he bestowed sight. And he answered
and said unto them, Go and tell John the things
which ye have seen and heard; the blind receive their
sight, the lame walk, the lepers are cleansed, and the
deaf hear, the dead are raised up, the poor have good
tidings preached to them. And blessed is he, who-

soever shall find no occasion of stumbling in me.
Luke 7: 18-23.

Was Jesus the Coming One? He did not quite measure up
to John's expectations. The Messiah was to purge the people
of evil elements, winnowing the chaff from the wheat and
burning it. His symbol was the axe. Jesus was manifesting
no such spirit. Was he then the Messiah?

Jesus shifted the test to another field. Human suffering
was being relieved and the poor were having glad news pro-
claimed to them. Sympathy for the people was the assured
common ground between Jesus and John. Jesus felt that
John would recognize the dawn of the reign of God by the
evidence which he offered him.

What, then, would be proper evidence that the reign of
God is gaining ground in our intellect and feeling?

THIRD DAY: *The Church, a Product of Social Feeling*

> And Jesus went about all the cities and the villages,
> teaching in their synagogues, and preaching the gos-
> pel of the kingdom, and healing all manner of disease
> and all manner of sickness. But when he saw the
> multitudes, he was moved with compassion for them,
> because they were distressed and scattered, as sheep
> not having a shepherd. Then saith he unto his dis-
> ciples, The harvest indeed is plenteous, but the labor-
> ers are few. Pray ye therefore the Lord of the
> harvest, that he send forth laborers into his harvest.
> And he called unto him his twelve disciples, and
> gave them authority over unclean spirits, to cast them
> out, and to heal all manner of disease and all man-
> ner of sickness.—Matt. 9:35-10:1.

The selection of the Twelve, their grouping by twos, and
their employment as independent messengers, was the most
important organizing act of Jesus. Out of it ultimately grew
the Christian Church. Now note what motives led to it.

Jesus was relieving social misery. He was oppressed by the sense of it. The Greek verbs are very inadequately rendered by "distressed and scattered." The first means "skinned, harried"; the second means "flung down, prostrate." The people were like a flock of sheep after the wolves are through with them. There was dearth of true leaders. So Jesus took the material he had and organized the apostolate—for what? The Church grew out of the social feeling of Jesus for the sufferings of the common people.

To what extent, in your judgment, does the Church today share the feeling of Jesus about the condition of the people and fulfil the purpose for which he organized the apostolate? Or has the condition of the people changed so that their social needs are less urgent?

FOURTH DAY: *Jesus Took Sides*

> And he lifted up his eyes on his disciples, and said, Blessed are ye poor: for yours is the kingdom of God. Blessed are ye that hunger now: for ye shall be filled. Blessed are ye that weep now: for ye shall laugh. Blessed are ye, when men shall hate you, and when they shall separate you from their company, and reproach you, and cast out your name as evil, for the Son of man's sake. Rejoice in that day, and leap for joy: for behold, your reward is great in heaven; for in the same manner did their fathers unto the prophets. But woe unto you that are rich! for ye have received your consolation. Woe unto you, ye that are full now! for ye shall hunger. Woe unto you, ye that laugh now! for ye shall mourn and weep. Woe unto you, when all men shall speak well of you! for in the same manner did their fathers to the false prophets.—Luke 6: 20-26.

In these Beatitudes, as Luke reports them, Jesus clearly takes sides with the lowly. He says God and the future are not on the side of the rich, the satiated, the devotees of pleasure, the people who take the popular side on everything.

Ultimately the verdict will be for those who are now poor and underfed, who carry the heavy end of things, and who have to stand for the unpopular side. In the report of the Beatitudes given by Matthew (5: 3-12) the terms are less social and more spiritual, and the contrast between the upper and lower classes is not marked; but even there the promise of the great reversal of things is to the humble and peaceable folk, the hard hit and unpopular; they are to inherit the earth, and also God's kingdom.

Would it make Jesus a wiser teacher and nobler figure if he had reversed his sympathies?

FIFTH DAY: *Salvation through the Common People*

In that same hour he rejoiced in the Holy Spirit, and said, I thank thee, O Father, Lord of heaven and earth, that thou didst hide these things from the wise and understanding, and didst reveal them unto babes: yea, Father; for so it was well-pleasing in thy sight.—Luke 10: 21.

For behold your calling, brethren, that not many wise after the flesh, not many mighty, not many noble, are called: but God chose the foolish things of the world, that he might put to shame them that are wise; and God chose the weak things of the world, that he might put to shame the things that are strong; and the base things of the world, and the things that are despised, did God choose, yea and the things that are not, that he might bring to nought the things that are: that no flesh should glory before God.— I Cor. 1: 26-29.

The actual results of his work proved to Jesus that his success was to be with the simple-minded, and not with the pundit class. He accepted the fact with a thrill of joy, and praised God for making it so. Paul verified the same alignment in the early Church. The upper classes held back through pride of birth or education, or through the timidity of wealth. In bringing in a new order of things, God had to use plain people to get a leverage.

What really was it that Jesus saw in the lowly to attract him?

SIXTH DAY: *Jesus, a Man of the People*

And when they drew nigh unto Jerusalem, and came unto Bethphage, unto the mount of Olives, then Jesus sent two disciples, saying unto them, Go into the village that is over against you, and straightway ye shall find an ass tied, and a colt with her: loose them, and bring them unto me. And if any one say aught unto you, ye shall say, The Lord hath need of them; and straightway he will send them. Now this is come to pass, that it might be fulfilled which was spoken through the prophet, saying,

Tell ye the daughter of Zion,

Behold, thy King cometh unto thee,

Meek, and riding upon an ass,

And upon a colt the foal of an ass.

And the disciples went, and did even as Jesus appointed them, and brought the ass, and the colt, and put on them their garments; and he sat thereon. And the most part of the multitude spread their garments in the way; and others cut branches from the trees, and spread them in the way. And the multitudes that went before him, and that followed, cried saying, Hosanna to the son of David: Blessed is he that cometh in the name of the Lord; Hosanna in the highest. And when he was come into Jerusalem, all the city was stirred, saying, Who is this? And the multitudes said, This is the prophet, Jesus, from Nazareth of Galilee.—Matt. 21: 1-11.

Here was a democratic procession! No caparisoned charger, but a burro—though a young and frisky one, carefully selected—no military escort with a brass band and a drum major, but a throng of peasants, shouting the psalms of their fathers and the hope of a good time coming; no costly rugs to carpet the way of the King, but the sweat-stained garments of working people and branches wrenched off by Galilæan fists. What was he, this King of the future, ridiculous or sublime?

If Jesus is ever to make his entry into the spiritual sovereignty of humanity, will the social classes line up as they did at Jerusalem?

SEVENTH DAY: *The Final Test for All*

But when the Son of man shall come in his glory, and all the angels with him, then shall he sit on the throne of his glory: and before him shall be gathered all the nations: and he shall separate them one from another, as the shepherd separateth the sheep from the goats; and he shall set the sheep on his right hand, but the goats on the left. Then shall the King say unto them on his right hand, Come, ye blessed of my Father, inherit the kingdom prepared for you from the foundation of the world: for I was hungry, and ye gave me to eat; I was thirsty, and ye gave me drink; I was a stranger, and ye took me in; naked, and ye clothed me; I was sick, and ye visited me; I was in prison, and ye came unto me. Then shall the righteous answer him, saying, Lord, when saw we thee hungry, and fed thee? or athirst, and gave thee drink? And when saw we thee a stranger, and took thee in? or naked, and clothed thee? And when saw we thee sick, or in prison, and came unto thee? And the King shall answer and say unto them, Verily I say unto you, Inasmuch as ye did it unto one of these my brethren, even these least, ye did it unto me. Then shall he say also unto them on the left hand, Depart from me, ye cursed, into the eternal fire which is prepared for the devil and his angels: for I was hungry, and ye did not give me to eat; I was thirsty, and ye gave me no drink; I was a stranger, and ye took me not in; naked, and ye clothed me not; sick, and in prison, and ye visited me

37

not. Then shall they also answer, saying, Lord, when saw we thee hungry, or athirst, or a stranger, or naked, or sick, or in prison, and did not minister unto thee? Then shall he answer them, saying, Verily I say unto you, Inasmuch as ye did it not unto one of these least, ye did it not unto me. And these shall go away into eternal punishment: but the righteous into eternal life.—Matt. 25: 31-46.

"Whence he shall come to judge the quick and the dead." Think of it—absolute justice done at last, by an all-knowing Judge, where no earthly pull of birth, wealth, learning, or power will count, and where all masks fall! By what code of law and what standard shall we be judged there? Here is the answer of Jesus: Not by creed and church questions, but by our human relations; by the reality of our social feeling; by our practical solidarity with our fellow-men. If we lived in the presence of hunger, loneliness, and oppression, in the same country with child labor, race contempt, the long day, rack rents, prostitution, just earnings withheld by power, the price of living raised to swell swollen profit— if we saw such things and remained apathetic, out we go.

You and I—to the right or the left?

STUDY FOR THE WEEK

No one can turn from a frank reading of the Gospels without realizing that Jesus had a deep fellow-feeling, not only for suffering and handicapped individuals, but for the mass of the poorer people of his country, the peasants, the fishermen, the artisans. He declared that it was his mission to bring glad tidings to this class; and not only glad words, but happy realities. Evidently the expectation of the coming Reign of God to his mind signified some substantial relief and release to the submerged and oppressed. Our modern human feeling glories in this side of our Saviour's work. Art and literature love to see him from this angle.

I

His concern for the poor was the necessary result of the two fundamental convictions discussed by us in the previous chapters. If he felt the sacredness of life even in its humble and hardworn forms, and if he felt the family unity of all men in such a way that the sorrows of the poor were his sorrows, then, of course, he could not be at ease while the people were "skinned and prostrate," "like sheep without a shepherd." Wherever any group has developed real solidarity, its best attention is always given to those who are most in need. "The whole have no need of a physician," said Jesus; the strong can take care of themselves.

So he cast in his lot with the people consciously. He slept in their homes, healed their diseases, ate their bread, and shared his own with them. He gave them a faith, a hope of better days, and a sense that God was on their side. Such a faith is more than meat and drink. In turn they rallied around him, and could not get enough of him. "The common people heard him gladly."

Furthermore, the feeling of Jesus for "the poor" was not the sort of compassion we feel for the hopelessly crippled in body or mind. His feeling was one of love and trust. The Galilæan peasants, from whom Peter and John sprang, were not morons, or the sodden dregs of city slums. They were the patient, hard-working folks who have always made up the rank and file of all peoples. They had their faults, and Jesus must have known them. But did he ever denounce them, or call them "offspring of vipers"? Did he ever indicate that their special vices were frustrating the Kingdom of God? They needed spiritual impulse and leadership, but their nature was sound and they were the raw material for the redeemed humanity which he strove to create.

II

There is one more quality which we shall have to recognize in the attitude of Jesus to "the poor." He saw them over against "the rich." Amid all the variations of human society these two groups always reappear—those who live by their own productive labor, and those who live on the productive labor of others whom they control. Practically they overlap and blend, but when our perspective is distant enough, we can distinguish them. In Greek and Roman society, in medieval life, and in all civilized nations of today—barring, of course, our own—we can see them side by side. Each conditions the other; neither would exist without the other. Each class develops its own moral and spiritual habits, its own set of virtues and vices. Some of us were born in the upper class, some in the lower; and in college groups the majority come from the border line. By instinct, by the experiences of life, or by national reflection, we usually give our moral allegiance to one or the other, and are then apt to lean to that side in every question arising.

Now, Jesus took sides with the group of toil. He stood up for them. He stood with them. We can not help seeing him with his arm thrown in protection about the poor man, and his other hand raised in warning to the rich. If we are in any doubt about this, we can let his contemporaries decide it for us. Plainly the common people claimed him as their friend. Did the governing classes have the same feeling for him? It seems hard to escape the conclusion that Jesus was not impartial between the two. Was he nevertheless just? To the æsthetic sense, and also to a superficial moral judgment, the upper classes are everywhere more congenial and attractive. To the moral judgment of Jesus, as we shall see more fully in a later chapter, there was something disquieting and dangerous about the spiritual qualities of "the rich," and something lovable and hopeful about the qualities of the common man. Was he right? This is a very important practical question for all who are disposed to follow his moral leadership.

The perception that Jesus championed the people can be found throughout literature and art. Our own Lowell has expressed it in his "Parable" in which he describes Jesus coming back to earth to see "how the men, my brethren, believe in me."

"Have ye founded your thrones and altars, then,
On the bodies and souls of living men?
And think ye that building shall endure,
Which shelters the noble and crushes the poor?

"With gates of silver and bars of gold
Ye have fenced my sheep from their Father's fold;
I have heard the dropping of their tears
In heaven these eighteen hundred years.

*　　*　　*

"Then Christ sought out an artisan,
A low-browed, stunted, haggard man,
And a motherless girl, whose fingers thin,
Pushed from her faintly want and sin.

"These set he in the midst of them,
And as they drew back their garment-hem
For fear of defilement, 'Lo, here,' said he,
'The images ye have made of me.'"

III

We shall get the historical setting for Christ's championship of the people by going back to the Old Testament prophets. They were his spiritual forebears. He nourished his mind on their writings and loved to quote them. Now, the Hebrew prophets with one accord stood up for the common people and laid the blame for social wrong on the powerful classes. They underlined no other sin with such scarlet marks as the sins of injustice, oppression, and the corruption of judges. But these are the sins which bear down the lowly, and have always been practiced and hushed up by the powerful. "Hear this word, ye kine of Bashan, that oppress the poor, that crush the needy. . . . Ye trample upon the poor, and take exactions from him of wheat; . . . ye that afflict the just, that take a bribe, and that turn aside the needy in the gate from their right. . . . For three transgressions of Israel, yea, for four, I will not turn away the punishment thereof; because they have sold the righteous for silver, and the needy for a pair of shoes; they that pant after the dust of the earth on the head of the poor" (Amos 4: 1; 5: 11-12; 2: 6-7). Micah describes the strong and crafty crowding the peasant from his ancestral holding and the mother from her home by the devices always used for such ends, exorbitant interest on loans, foreclosure in times of distress, "seeing the judge" before the trial, and hardness of heart toward broken life and happiness (Micah 2: 1-2; 2: 9; 3: 1-2). We cannot belittle the moral insight of that unique succession of men. Their spiritual force is still hard at work in our Christian civilization, especially in the contribution which the Jewish people are making to the labor movement.

IV

Among the Greeks and Romans political and literary life was so completely dominated by the aristocratic class that no such succession of champions of the common man could well arise. Yet some of the men of whom posterity thinks with most veneration were upper-class champions of the common people—Solon, for instance, Manlius, and the Gracchi.

In recent centuries the vast forces of social evolution seem to have set in the direction toward which Jesus faced. Since the Reformation the institutions of religion have been more or less democratized. The common people have secured some participation in political power and have been able to use it somewhat for their economic betterment. They share much more fully in education than formerly. Before the outbreak of the Great War it seemed safe to anticipate that the working people would secure an increasing share of the social wealth, the security, the opportunities for health, for artistic enjoyment, and of all that makes life worth living. Today the future is heavily clouded and uncertain; but our faith still holds that even the great disaster will help ultimately to weaken the despotic and exploiting forces, and make the condition of the common people more than ever the chief concern of science and statesmanship.

Jesus was on the side of the common people long before democracy was on the ascendant. He loved them, felt their worth, trusted their latent capacities, and promised them the Kingdom of God. The religion he founded, even when impure and under the control of the upper classes, has been the historical basis for the aspirations of the common people and has readily united with democratic movements. His personality and spirit has remained an impelling and directing force in the minds of many individuals who have "gone to the people" because they know Jesus is with them. In fact we can look for more direct social effectiveness of Jesus in the future, because the new historical interpretation of the Bible helps us to see him more plainly amid the social life of his own people.

V

So we must add a third social principle to the first two. The first was that life and personality are sacred; the second that men belong together; the third is that the strong must stand with the weak and defend their cause. In his description of the Messianic Judgment, Jesus proposed to recognize as his followers only those who had responded to the call of human need and solidarity. He created the apostleship and therewith the germ of the Church in order to serve the people whose needs he saw and felt.

How does this concern college men and women? By our opportunities and equipment we rank with the strong. Disciplined intellect is armor and sword. Many of us have inherited social standing and some wealth; it may not be much, but it raises us above the terrible push of immediate need. What relation do we propose to have with the great mass of men and women who were born without the chances which have

fallen to us without exertion? Do we propose to serve them
or to ride on them? Will we seek to gain some form of
power by means of which we can live in plenty, with only
slight and pleasurable exertion? In that case we can hardly
return to our fellow-men in work as much as we take from
them in enjoyment and luxury. We shall be part of that
dead weight which has always bent the back of the poor.
Is that an honorable ambition? Or do we propose to enter
the working team of humanity and to hold up our end? Our
end ought to be heavier than the average because we have
had longer and better training. "To whomsoever much is
given, of him shall much be required."

The moral problem for college communities is accentuated
when we remember that few students pay fully for what
they get. Whether our institutions are supported from taxa-
tion or from endowments, a large part of their incomes are
derived from the annual labor of society; tuitions pay only
a fraction of the running expenses and of the interest on the
plant. Even if a student pays all charges, he is in part a
pensioner on the public. The working people in the last
resort support us; the same people who are often so eager
for education, and who can not get it. Some of them would
feel rich if they had the leavings of knowledge which we
throw to the floor and tread upon in our spirit of surfeit.
To take our education at their hands and use it to devise
ways by which we can continue to live on them, seems disquieting even to a pagan conscience. It ought to be in-
sufferable to a sense of social responsibility trained under
Christian influences.

Here is a test for college communities more searching than
the physical test of athletics, or the intellectual tests of
scholarship. Do we feel our social unity with the people who
work for their living, and do we propose to use our special
privileges and capacities for their social redemption?

"When wilt Thou save the people?
    O God of Mercy, when?

Not kings and lords, but nations,
Not thrones and crowns, but men.
Flowers of Thy heart, O' God, are they.
Let them not pass like weeds away,
Let them not fade in sunless day!
God save the people!"—EBENEZER ELLIOTT.

SUGGESTIONS FOR THOUGHT AND DISCUSSION

I. *The Partisanship of Jesus*

1. Did Jesus really take sides with the poor? Prove it.
2. Try to prove the other side.
3. Which would be safer evidence: single sayings, or the total impression of his life and teachings?
4. What do you conclude regarding the attitude of Jesus?

II. *The Church and the People*

1. What motives led Jesus to organize and send out the twelve? What was the historical significance of that action?
2. When and how did the Church lose its working class character?
3. Does the Church today share Jesus' feelings about the condition of the people? Sum up evidence for and against.
4. What is the true function of the Church in society so far as the poor are concerned?

III. *Standing up for the People Today*

1. Is it a superficial or profound test to range a man according to his sympathy with the common people?
2. What does it involve to stand up for the people today? How does it differ from charity and relief work?
3. Name some men and women in our own times who seem to have stood up for them most wisely and effectively.
4. What are the vices of social reformers?

IV. *The Concern of College Men and Women*

1. How can college men and women make a just return for their special opportunities?

✓ 2. What movements in college and university life in recent years are in line with this social principle of Jesus?

3. What part have the university students of Russia, Austria, Germany, and England taken in social movements? Have American students ever taken a similar interest in working class movements? If not, why not?

V. *For Special Discussion*

1. Is it an advantage or disadvantage to Christianity that it began among the working class? What effects did that have on its ethical points of view and its impulses?

2. Why did the regeneration of ancient society have to come through the lowly? Will it have to come the same way today?

3. Is it ethical to live without productive labor? Is it morally tolerable to enjoy excessive leisure purchased by the excessive toil of others?

4. Is there any clear conviction on this question in the Christian Church today?

5. Is the fact that a person has sprung from the working-class a guarantee that he will have the working-class sympathies?

6. Who seem to have more natural democratic feeling, the men or the women of the upper classes?

12-1-19

PART II

THE SOCIAL IDEAL OF JESUS

CHAPTER IV

THE KINGDOM OF GOD: ITS VALUES

The Right Social Order is the Highest Good for All

The first three chapters dealt with simple human principles which are common and instinctive with all real men. Jesus simply expanded the range of their application, clarified our comprehension of them, placed them in the very center of religious duty, and so lifted them to the high level of great social and religious principles.

In the next three chapters we shall take up a conception which is not universally human, but which Jesus derived from the historic life of the Hebrew people—the idea of the "Kingdom of God." A better translation would be "the Reign of God." This conception embodied the social ideal and purpose of the best minds of one of the few creative nations of history.

How did Jesus interpret this inherited social ideal? What did the Kingdom of God seem to him to offer men? What did it demand of them? What immediate ethical duty did this social ideal involve? Our inquiry will move along these lines in the next three chapters.

DAILY READINGS

FIRST DAY: *The Main Chance*

The kingdom of heaven is like unto a treasure hidden in the field; which a man found, and hid; and in his joy he goeth and selleth all that he hath, and buyeth that field.

Again, the kingdom of heaven is like unto a man that is a merchant seeking goodly pearls: and having

found one pearl of great price, he went and sold
all that he had, and bought it.—Matt. 13: 44-46.

Teres of diamonds

When war was common, property insecure, and safe de-
posit vaults were scarce, it was common for men to bury
treasure in time of trouble and to forget it when they were
dead. Whoever accidentally found it "struck pay dirt" and
hastened to locate his claim. An extraordinary jewel, too,
was a bonanza. The infant capitalists of that day were wise
enough to liquidate their other holdings and invest everything in the main chance. Jesus calls for the application of
the same method on the higher level. The Kingdom of God
is the highest good of all; why not stake all on the chance
of that? These parables were spoken out of his own experience. He was gladly surrendering home, comfort, public
approval, and life itself to realize the Reign of God in
humanity.

Imagine that Jesus had surrendered his religious idealism,
had gained wealth and official standing, and died of old age.
Would he have gained? What would the world have lost?

Second Day: *The Master Fact*

From that time began Jesus to preach, and to say,
Repent ye; for the kingdom of heaven is at hand.
—Matt. 4: 17.

The Kingdom of God is a master fact. It takes control.
When the Kingdom becomes a reality to us, we can not live
on in the old way. We must repent, begin over, overhaul
the values of life and put them down at their true price,
and so readjust our fundamental directions. The conduct of
the individual must rise in response to higher conceptions of
the meaning and possibilities of the life of humanity. Tolstoi
has described his conversion in the simplest terms in the
introduction to "My Religion:"

"Five years ago faith came to me; I believed in

50

the doctrine of Jesus, and my whole life underwent a sudden transformation. What I had once wished for I wished for no longer, and I began to desire what I had never desired before. What had once appeared to me right now became wrong, and the wrong of the past I beheld as right. My condition was like that of a man who goes forth upon some errand, and having traversed a portion of the road, decides that the matter is of no importance, and turns back. What was at first on his right hand is now on his left, and what was at his left hand is now on his right; instead of going away from his abode, he desires to get back to it as soon as possible. My life and my desires were completely changed; good and evil interchanged meanings. Why so? Because I understood the doctrine of Jesus in a different way from that in which I had understood it before." . . . "I understood the words of Jesus, and life and death ceased to be evil; instead of despair, I tasted joy and happiness."

Some seek religion to escape hell and attain heaven; some to attain a perfect personality; some to bring in the Reign of God. Give cases. Estimate the relative religious and social significance of these different spiritual experiences.

THIRD DAY: *Baptism and the New Order*

> Even as it is written in Isaiah the prophet,
> Behold, I send my messenger before thy face,
> Who shall prepare thy way;
> The voice of one crying in the wilderness,
> Make ye ready the way of the Lord,
> Make his paths straight;

John came, who baptized in the wilderness and preached the baptism of repentance unto remission of sins. And there went out unto him all the country of Judæa, and all they of Jerusalem; and they were baptized of him in the river Jordan, confessing their sins. And John was clothed with camel's hair, and had a leathern girdle about his loins, and did eat

51

locusts and wild honey. And he preached, saying,
There cometh after me he that is mightier than I,
the latchet of whose shoes I am not worthy to stoop
down and unloose. I baptized you in water; but he
shall baptize you in the Holy Spirit.—Mark 1:2-8.

The men who were baptized by John were not looking
forward to death and to salvation after death, but to the
coming of the Kingdom of God and of his Messiah. They
repented and accepted the badge of baptism in order to have
a share in the blessings of the Kingdom and to escape the
imminent judgment of the Messiah. Baptism was then
the mark of a national and social movement toward a new
era, and was a personal dedication to a righteous social
order. This original idea of baptism was practically lost
to the Christian consciousness in later times. Every man
who today realizes the Kingdom of God as the supreme good,
can reaffirm his own baptism as a dedication to the social
ideal and to the leadership of Jesus who initiated it. Such
a social interpretation of our personal discipleship will bring
us into closer spiritual agreement with the original aim of
Christianity.

Has our baptism ever had a social significance to us?

FOURTH DAY: *The Way to Happiness*

Therefore I say unto you, Be not anxious for
your life, what ye shall eat, or what ye shall drink;
nor yet for your body, what ye shall put on. Is not
the life more than the food, and the body than the
raiment? Behold the birds of the heaven, that they
sow not, neither do they reap, nor gather into barns,
and your heavenly Father feedeth them. Are not
ye of much more value than they? And which of
you by being anxious can add one cubit unto the
measure of his life? And why are ye anxious concerning raiment? Consider the lilies of the field,
how they grow; they toil not, neither do they spin:
yet I say unto you, that even Solomon in all his

glory was not arrayed like one of these. But if God doth so clothe the grass of the field, which to-day is, and to-morrow is cast into the oven, shall he not much more clothe you, O ye of little faith? Be not therefore anxious, saying, What shall we eat? or, What shall we drink? or, Wherewithal shall we be clothed? For after all these things do the Gentiles seek; for your heavenly Father knoweth that ye have need of all these things. But seek ye first his kingdom, and his righteousness; and all these things shall be added unto you. Be not therefore anxious for the morrow: for the morrow will be anxious for itself. Sufficient unto the day is the evil thereof.
—Matt. 6: 25-34.

This is a song of divine carelessness; not the recklessness of a tramp who has lost his self-respect and his capacity for long outlooks, but the carelessness of an aristocratic spirit, conscious of his high human dignity. God has given us life; will he not give what life needs? If the birds and the lilies can make a living, can not we? It is pagan and low-bred to wear out our souls with worry about minor needs.

The key to this passage lies in the words "your Father," and "his Kingdom." Man is a child of God, and that dignity gives some calm and assurance amid the worries of life. If we set our life toward the Kingdom as the supreme aim, all the lesser interests will drop to their proper place. In the measure in which the will of God is done and his righteousness practiced among men, the satisfaction of the main material wants will be easy. The Kingdom, the true social order, is the highest good; all other good things are contained in it.

To worry or not to worry, that is the question. *Have we ever tried the adoption of a high aim as the way to happiness?*

FIFTH DAY: *Sunny Religion*

And John's disciples and the Pharisees were fasting: and they come and say unto him, Why do

53

John's disciples and the disciples of the Pharisees fast,
but thy disciples fast not? And Jesus said unto
them, Can the sons of the bridechamber fast, while
the bridegroom is with them? as long as they have
the bridegroom with them, they cannot fast. But
the days will come, when the bridegroom shall be
taken away from them, and then will they fast in
that day. No man seweth a piece of undressed cloth
on an old garment: else that which should fill it up
taketh from it, the new from the old, and a worse
rent is made. And no man putteth new wine into
old wine-skins; else the wine will burst the skins, and
the wine perisheth, and the skins: but they put new
wine into fresh wine-skins.—Mark 2: 18-22.

Fasting was an important part of piety with strict Jews.
It was an expression of religious sorrow and self-abasement.
Afflicting the body intensified this spiritual emotion. The
disciples of the Pharisees and of John were surprised and
shocked by the fact that Jesus and his group disregarded this
custom. The reply of Jesus shows the religious temper of
Jesus in a new light. He says his disciples are happy,
like guests at a wedding; why should they act as if they
were mournful? Fasting was alien to the spirit which ruled
in his company. It would be just as inappropriate as to
patch a piece of unshrunken stuff on an old garment, or to
put fermenting wine in old and brittle skin bottles. The
religion of Jesus, then, was distinguished from other earnest
religion by its happy and sunny character. See also the sharp
distinction he makes between the ascetic life of John and his
own enjoyment of social life (Matt. 11: 16-19). Yet Jesus
was a homeless man, moving toward death.

There seems to be a difference between the self-denial of
ascetic religion, and the surrender of self to the Kingdom of
God. What is it?

SIXTH DAY: *The Poise of Expectancy*

Then shall the kingdom of heaven be likened unto
ten virgins, who took their lamps, and went forth

to meet the bridegroom. And five of them were foolish, and five were wise. For the foolish, when they took their lamps, took no oil with them: but the wise took oil in their vessels with their lamps. Now while the bridegroom tarried, they all slumbered and slept. But at midnight there is a cry, Behold, the bridegroom! Come ye forth to meet him. Then all those virgins arose, and trimmed their lamps. And the foolish said unto the wise, Give us of your oil; for our lamps are going out. But the wise answered, saying, Peradventure there will not be enough for us and you: go ye rather to them that sell, and buy for yourselves. And while they went away to buy, the bridegroom came; and they that were ready went in with him to the marriage feast: and the door was shut. Afterward came also the other virgins, saying, Lord, Lord, open to us. But he answered and said, Verily I say unto you, I know you not. Watch therefore, for ye know not the day nor the hour.—Matt. 25: 1-13.

The Lord was to return soon and consummate the establishment of his Kingdom. The first two generations of Christians took this hope very seriously. Expectancy was the true pose of Christians. Under the conditions of that time this was their way of declaring that the Kingdom of God is the highest good and that all our life should be concentrated on it. If Jesus lived today he could find even more effective exhortations to look sharp and not get left. But is the constant expectation of a divine catastrophe from heaven possible for modern minds? Must we translate that expectation into the hope of moral and social development? By doing so, can we still have a religious sense of a great and divine future overhanging humanity which will give to our life the same value and solemnity which the first generation felt?

Explain what a strong social hope and faith would contribute to a person's life in the course of years.

How do faith and practical social effort react on each other?

SEVENTH DAY: *The Coming Joys*

> Blessed are the meek: for they shall inherit the earth.
>
> Blessed are they that hunger and thirst after righteousness: for they shall be filled.
>
> Blessed are the merciful: for they shall obtain mercy.
>
> Blessed are the pure in heart: for they shall see God.
>
> Blessed are the peacemakers: for they shall be called sons of God.
>
> Blessed are they that have been persecuted for righteousness' sake: for theirs is the kingdom of heaven.—Matt. 5: 5-10.

In the Sermon on the Mount Jesus formally outlined his conceptions of ethical and religious life as distinguished from those then current. It was the platform of the Kingdom of God. We might expect it to begin with denunciation. Instead it opens with a spontaneous burst of joy. A great good was coming. It would bring a store of blessings to all who had the inward qualifications to receive them. All who felt the divine dissatisfaction with themselves and the craving for social justice and righteousness, would get their satisfaction (v. 3, 4, 6). The higher social virtues, gentleness, purity of heart, peaceableness, would get recognition and gain ascendancy (v. 5, 7, 8, 9). But the climax of praise and promise is for those who propagated righteousness where it was not wanted, and suffered for it (v. 10-12). "These words belong to the greatest ever uttered" (Hegel). They are pure religion, and they were called forth by religious faith in a social ideal.

Have we known men and women who had some of these qualities, who lived within the Kingdom of God, and who enjoyed its blessings? If they have ennobled our life, let us think of them a moment with a silent benediction.

STUDY FOR THE WEEK

We see from the passages we have studied that the mind of Jesus was centered on a great hope which was just ahead. It was so beautiful that even in anticipation it was filling his soul with joy and he knew it would bless all who shared in it. It seemed to him so valuable and engrossing that a man ought to stake his whole life on attaining it, and subordinate all other aims to this dominant desire.

I

He spoke of this great good as "the Kingdom of God." Even a superficial reading of the first three Gospels shows that this was the pivot of his teaching. Yet he nowhere defines the phrase. He took an understanding of it for granted with his hearers, and simply announced that it was now close at hand, and they must act accordingly. What did the words mean to them? The idea covered by the phrase was an historic product of the Jewish people, and we shall have to understand it as such.

The Hebrew prophets had concentrated their incomparable religious energy on the simple demand for righteousness, especially in social and national life. The actual life of the nation, especially of its ruling classes, of course never squared with the religious ideal. The injustice and oppression around them seemed intolerable to the prophets, just because the ethical imperative within them was so strong. So their unsatisfied desire for righteousness took the form of an ardent expectation of a coming day when things would be as they ought to be. God would make bare his holy arm to punish the wicked, to sift the good, to establish his law, and to vindicate the rights of the oppressed. This great "day of Jehovah" would inaugurate a new age, the Kingdom of God, the Reign of God. The phrase, then, embodies the social ideal of the finest religious minds of a unique people. The essential thing in it is the projection into the future of the demand for a just social order. The prophets looked to a direct miraculous act of God to realize their vision, but they were in close touch with the facts of political life and always demanded social action on the human side.

Plato's Republic and More's Utopia are intellectual productions which have appealed to single idealistic minds. The Hebrew prophets succeeded in socializing their ideal. By the force of religion they wrought the conception of the Kingdom of God into the common mind of a nation as a traditional conviction which was assimilated by every new generation.

But when a great idea is appropriated by the masses, it is sure to become cruder to suit their intellect and their need; and when a national ideal is handed on for centuries, it will change with the changing fortunes of the people that holds it. When the Hebrew nation came under the foreign rule of the Assyrians, Persians, and finally the Romans, its freedom and chance for political action were lost, and its political ideals, too, deteriorated. The Kingdom hope became theological, artificial, a scheme of epochs of predetermined length and of marvelous stage settings. Yet, even in this form, it was a splendid hope of emancipation, of national greatness, and of future justice and fraternity, and it helped to keep the nation's soul alive amid crushing sorrows.

The people at the time of Jesus in the main held this apocalyptic conception of the Kingdom. It was to come as a divine catastrophe, beginning with an act of judgment and resulting in a glorious Jewish imperialism. Jesus shared the substance of the expectation, but as a true spiritual leader he reconstructed, clarified, and elevated the hope of the masses. He would have nothing to do with any plans involving bloodshed and force revolution. The Hebrew Jehovah became "our Father in heaven" and this democratized the Reign of Jehovah. The pious Jew expected God to enforce the ceremonial laws; Jesus had little to say about religious ceremonial, and a great deal about righteousness and love. Under his hands the Jewish imperialistic dream changed into a call for universal human fraternity. He repeatedly and emphatically explained the coming of the Kingdom in terms taken

58

from biological growth, and his thoughts seem to have verged away from the popular catastrophic ideas toward ideas of organic development. These changes—if we have correctly interpreted them—represent Jesus' own contribution to the history of the Kingdom ideal, and they are all in the same direction in which the modern mind has moved. (For a fuller statement of these modifications see Rauschenbusch, "Christianizing the Social Order," p. 48-68.)

II

So much by way of historical information. Now let us emphasize again that this social ideal seemed to Jesus so fair and fine that he gave his whole soul to it. Naturally he would. Since he loved men and believed in their solidarity, the conception of a God-filled humanity living in a righteous social order, which would give free play to love and would bind all in close ties, would be the only satisfying outlook for him. He promised that all who hungered and thirsted after righteousness would be satisfied in the Kingdom, and he was himself the chief of these. The Kingdom of God was his fatherland, in which his spirit lived with God; and with that vision of perfect humanity before him, he kept its calm and tranquillity amid the enmity of men as he sought to win men to its better ways.

The Kingdom of God is the highest good. The idea of God is the highest and most comprehensive conception in philosophy; the idea of the Kingdom of God is the highest and broadest idea in sociology and ethics. It is so high and broad that many find it hard even to grasp the idea. Just as a barbaric tribe of hunters or fishermen would find it impossible to comprehend the social coherence and the patriotism of a nation of a hundred millions; just as the narrow nationalist of today falls down intellectually and morally when he confronts world-forces and relations: so we who are trained to think in terms of family and State, give out when we are to treat the Kingdom of God as a reality. It takes faith of the intellect to comprehend a stage of evolution before it is reached. It takes faith of character to launch yourself toward a great moral goal before its tangible and profitable elements are within reach. It takes more moral daring today than for a century past to believe in the reemergence and final victory of God's social order. But this is the time for all true believers to square their shoulders and say with Galileo, "And yet it moves."

Any man whose soul is kindled by the conception of the Kingdom of God is a real man. Whoever loves the idea, must turn it into reality as far as life lets him. Whoever tries it, will suffer. But even if he suffers, he will be more blessed and more truly a man than he would be if he did not try. In seeking the Kingdom he realizes himself. "He that loseth his life for my sake, shall find it."

III

Jesus bade us "seek first the Kingdom of God and his righteousness," and he obeyed his own call. The main object of his life was the ideal social order and the perfect ethic. Now if Jesus is our ideal of human goodness, is any goodness good unless it works in the same direction? If a man is of flawless private life, but is indifferent to any social ideal, or even hostile to all attempts at better justice and greater fraternity, is he really good? Even a strong desire for personal perfection, if there is no desire for a regeneration of society in it, must be rated as sub-Christian because it is lacking in the sense of solidarity and may be lacking in love.

SUGGESTIONS FOR THOUGHT AND DISCUSSION

I. *The Power of a Great Idea*

1. Did the idea of the Kingdom of God ever play a part in your religious education?
2. Did you feel any response to it in studying this lesson? Does it have reality?

3. Suppose an entire study group should fail to see anything in it, would that prove it valueless?

II. *Historical Changes in the Kingdom Ideal*

1. How did the Kingdom ideal take shape in the minds of the Hebrew prophets?

2. Explain the nature of the apocalyptic hope and its divergence from the prophetic ideal.

3. What passages seem to throw the most light on Jesus' conception of it, and his feeling about it? What do you think about the Beatitudes from this point of view?

4. At what points did Jesus clarify and elevate the hereditary hope of his nation? Summarize the conception of the Kingdom as it lay in the mind of Jesus.

III. *Present Possibilities of the Kingdom Idea*

1. What value would the preaching of the Kingdom of God have in evangelistic work today?

2. How would it affect religious education and the moral outlook of the young?

3. How would the possession of the Kingdom faith equip the Church for leadership in an age of social movements and unrest?

4. How does the Kingdom hope add to the joyousness of the Christian life?

5. How does Jesus' conception of the Kingdom of God connect with the great social and national hopes of today?

IV. *For Special Discussion*

1. How does a man realize himself in seeking the Kingdom? How does a man realize the Kingdom in developing himself?

2. Does the idea seem to offer a religious vehicle for conceptions you have derived from sociological work?

3. Does a social concept like the "Kingdom of God" gain

anything for its practical efficiency today from being ancient, and from being religious?

4. Will such a concept ever be effective with the masses unless it is essentially religious?

CHAPTER V

THE KINGDOM OF GOD: ITS TASKS

The Right Social Order is the Supreme Task for Each

The perfect social order is the highest good. In so far as it is a gift of God, offered to the individual like the fertile earth and the oxygen of the air, we must appropriate it and enjoy every approximation to the perfect society. But what is the responsibility of the individual toward the achievement of the ideal social order? What task does it lay on him? How did Jesus see this problem? It is finely stated in the words with which Émile de Laveleye closes his book "Sur la propriété": "There is a social order which is the best. Necessarily it is not always the present order. Else why should we seek to change the latter? But it is that order which ought to exist to realize the greatest good for humanity. God knows it and wills it. It is for man to discover and establish it."

What, then, is the responsibility of the individual with regard to the achievement of this highest good?

DAILY READINGS

FIRST DAY: *The Kingdom of Hard Work*

For it is as when a man, going into another country, called his own servants, and delivered unto them his goods. And unto one he gave five talents, to another two, to another one; to each according to his several ability; and he went on his journey. Straightway he that received the five talents went and traded with them, and made other five talents.

In like manner he also that received the two gained other two. But he that received the one went away and digged in the earth, and hid his lord's money. Now after a long time the lord of those servants cometh, and maketh a reckoning with them. And he that received the five talents came and brought other five talents, saying, Lord, thou deliveredst unto me five talents: lo, I have gained other five talents. His lord said unto him, Well done, good and faithful servant: thou hast been faithful over a few things, I will set thee over many things; enter thou into the joy of thy lord. And he also that received the two talents came and said, Lord, thou deliveredst unto me two talents: lo, I have gained other two talents. His lord said unto him, Well done, good and faithful servant: thou hast been faithful over a few things, I will set thee over many things; enter thou into the joy of thy lord. And he also that had received the one talent came and said, Lord, I knew thee that thou art a hard man, reaping where thou didst not sow, and gathering where thou didst not scatter; and I was afraid, and went away and hid thy talent in the earth: lo, thou hast thine own. But his lord answered and said unto him, Thou wicked and slothful servant, thou knewest that I reap where I sowed not, and gather where I did not scatter; thou oughtest therefore to have put my money to the bankers, and at my coming I should have received back mine own with interest. Take ye away therefore the talent from him, and give it unto him that hath the ten talents. For unto every one that hath shall be given, and he shall have abundance: but from him that hath not, even that which he hath shall be taken away. And cast ye out the unprofitable servant into the outer darkness: there shall be the weeping and the gnashing of teeth.
—Matt. 25: 14-30.

Evidently the sympathy of Jesus was with the two men who hustled, and not with the fellow who took it out in growling and blaming the boss. Jesus would have agreed to the proposition that to live an unproductive life is one of the cardinal sins. Evolution and Christianity agree on that. This exhortation to do good work was given when Jesus was looking forward to his death and his absence. He would leave the Kingdom of God as an unfinished task. He wanted his disciples to carry forward their Master's business under their own initiative when he was not there to direct them. The new conditions would throw even heavier responsibilities on them.

Can you translate this parable into terms of college life and sketch three college students as companion pieces to the three business men?

SECOND DAY: *The Call to Action*

And passing along by the sea of Galilee, he saw Simon and Andrew the brother of Simon casting a net in the sea; for they were fishers. And Jesus said unto them, Come ye after me, and I will make you to become fishers of men. And straightway they left the nets, and followed him. And going on a little further, he saw James the son of Zebedee, and John his brother, who also were in the boat mending the nets. And straightway he called them: and they left their father Zebedee in the boat with the hired servants, and went after him.—Mark 1: 16-20.

And as Jesus passed by from thence, he saw a man, called Matthew, sitting at the place of toll: and he saith unto him, Follow me. And he arose and followed him.—Matt. 9: 9.

And as they went on the way, a certain man said unto him, I will follow thee whithersoever thou goest. And Jesus said unto him, The foxes have holes, and the birds of the heaven have nests; but the Son of man hath not where to lay his head. And he said unto another, Follow me. But he said, Lord, suffer me first to go and bury my father.

65

But he said unto him, Leave the dead to bury their own dead; but go thou and publish abroad the kingdom of God. And another also said, I will follow thee, Lord; but first suffer me to bid farewell to them that are at my house. But Jesus said unto him, No man, having put his hand to the plow, and looking back, is fit for the kingdom of God.—Luke 9: 57-62.

The way in which Jesus called his disciples shows that he felt he had a big business in hand. It was a call to action, to conflict and loss, and there was snap in it. Leaving their boats and nets doubtless seemed a big proposition to these four fishermen; but they did it. Matthew had to give up a government job with pickings. These five rose to their chance with courageous decision, and their names are still borne by millions of boys today. The names of the other three are lost to fame. One of them gushed and Jesus cooled off his emotions. The second and third wanted to procrastinate and hid behind social obligations. Note that epigram about the ploughman. It is a splendid expression of intelligent and concentrated energy. You can't drive a straight furrow while you "rubber." You've got to "tend to your job."

Four of the first five are said to have died a violent death. Would they have been wiser if they had looked out for Number One?

THIRD DAY: *The Futility of Talk*

Not every one that saith unto me, Lord, Lord, shall enter into the kingdom of heaven; but he that doeth the will of my Father who is in heaven. Many will say to me in that day, Lord, Lord, did we not prophesy by thy name, and by thy name cast out demons, and by thy name do many mighty works? And then will I profess unto them, I never knew you: depart from me, ye that work iniquity. Every one therefore that heareth these words of mine, and doeth them, shall be likened unto a wise man, who built his house upon the rock: and the rain descended, and the floods came, and the winds blew, and beat upon that house; and it fell not: for it was founded upon the rock. And every one that heareth these words of mine, and doeth them not, shall be likened unto a foolish man, who built his house upon the sand: and the rain descended, and the floods came, and the winds blew, and smote upon that house; and it fell: and great was the fall thereof.—Matt. 7: 21-27.

Jesus evidently felt deeply the emptiness and futility of much of the religious talk. He was interested only in those emotions and professions which could get themselves translated into character and action. Words have always been the bane of religion as well as its vehicle. Religious emotion has enormous motive force, but it is the easiest thing in the world for it to sizzle away in high professions and wordy prayers. In that case it is a substitute and counterfeit, and a damage to the Reign of God among men.

How about our own religious talk?

Would it be better, then, to give up preaching and public prayer?

What has the utterance of religion done for us?

FOURTH DAY: *This Camel Passed Through*

And he entered and was passing through Jericho. And behold, a man called by name Zacchæus; and he was a chief publican, and he was rich. And he sought to see Jesus who he was; and could not for the crowd, because he was little of stature. And he ran on before, and climbed up into a sycomore tree to see him: for he was to pass that way. And when Jesus came to the place, he looked up, and said unto him, Zacchæus, make haste, and come down; for to-day I must abide at thy house. And he made haste, and came down, and received him joyfully. And when they saw it, they all murmured, saying,

He is gone in to lodge with a man that is a sinner.
And Zacchæus stood, and said unto the Lord, Behold, Lord, the half of my goods I give to the poor;
and if I have wrongfully exacted aught of any man,
I restore fourfold. And Jesus said unto him, To-day
is salvation come to this house, forasmuch as he also
is a son of Abraham. For the Son of man came to
seek and to save that which was lost.—Luke 19: 1-10.

Zacchæus was engaged in the profitable but shady business of farming the Roman taxing system in one of the
richest districts of Palestine. He was a politician and business man combined, and the kind of man that is "bound to
land." Being only five feet one he had no chance amid
a crowd in a narrow street watching a procession. So he
climbed a tree. Imagine a corporation president climbing
a telegraph post to see Jesus! This spirit of determination
appealed to Jesus and he promptly made friends with him,
though he well knew he would lose some more of his reputation by identifying himself with a publican. Zacchæus
proved his fitness for the Kingdom of God by parting with
his accumulated graft at a single sweep. Fifty per cent
of his property given away outright; the balance used to
make restitution at the rate of four hundred per cent—how
much was left? Here a camel passed through the needle's
eye, and Jesus stood and cheered.

At what points is the moral energy of college men and
women most severely tested? Where do they meet their
great spiritual decisions? *Life choices?*

Fifth Day: *Will in Prayer*

And he spake a parable unto them to the end that
they ought always to pray, and not to faint; saying,
There was in a city a judge, who feared not God,
and regarded not man: and there was a widow in
that city; and she came oft unto him, saying, Avenge
me of mine adversary. And he would not for a
while: but afterward he said within himself, Though

68

I fear not God, nor regard man; yet because this widow troubleth me, I will avenge her, lest she wear me out by her continual coming. And the Lord said, Hear what the unrighteous judge saith. And shall not God avenge his elect, that cry to him day and night, and yet he is longsuffering over them?—Luke 18: 1-7.

In most of his sayings on prayer Jesus either objected to the wordiness of prayers (Matt. 6: 5-13), or he demanded more will and persistence. In the story of the widow and the judge the odds were against the widow. Being only a widow she had no pull and no vote. The judge was frankly a tough case, untouched by religion and conscience, and thick-skinned as to public opinion. Yet the widow won out by sheer doggedness. Surely the mind that sketched the reiterating widow and the collapsing politician had an admiring eye for energy of action. Jesus wanted that spirit and determination put into prayer. But note that he was thinking, not of personal edification, nor of private benefits to be obtained, but of the "avenging of God's elect"; that is, of straightening out the affairs of the world so that the wrongs of the righteous would be redressed. A keen social consciousness about the condition of God's people, coupled with "hunger and thirst for justice," can turn prayer into action.

Have we any experience of prayer concentrated on great public evils? How does that differ from prayers centering about our own interests? (See Fosdick, "The Meaning of Prayer," Chapter X.)

SIXTH DAY: *Twelve against the Field*

And as ye go, preach, saying, The kingdom of heaven is at hand. Heal the sick, raise the dead, cleanse the lepers, cast out demons: freely ye received, freely give. Get you no gold, nor silver, nor brass in your purses: no wallet for your journey, neither two coats, nor shoes, nor staff: for the laborer is worthy of his food. And into whatsoever city or village ye shall enter, search out who in it is worthy; and there abide till ye go forth. . . . And whosoever shall not receive you, nor hear your words, as ye go forth out of that house or that city, shake off the dust of your feet. Verily I say unto you, It shall be more tolerable for the land of Sodom and Gomorrah in the day of judgment, than for that city. . . . And be not afraid of them that kill the body, but are not able to kill the soul.— Matt. 10: 7-11, 14-15, 28a.

This whole chapter expresses with immense vitality the heroic spirit called forth by the Kingdom propaganda. Jesus sent these twelve men through the villages of Galilee to duplicate and multiply what he was doing. The natural leaders of society, the able, the educated, the powerful, were concerned in setting up their own kingdom and enslaving their fellows to serve them. So Jesus took what material he had, peasants and fishermen, and created a new leadership. He flung them against existing society, knowing well that they would have to face opposition. In fact, they were destined, one by one, to go to death for their cause. He tells them not to mind a little thing like death, but to do their work and rally the people around the idea of the Reign of God.

Can the men and women who are today trying to rebuild human society on a basis of social justice and fraternity claim any right of succession in the sending of the Twelve?

SEVENTH DAY: *Doing All, and Then Some*

But who is there of you, having a servant plowing or keeping sheep, that will say unto him, when he is come in from the field, Come straightway and sit down to meat; and will not rather say unto him, Make ready wherewith I may sup, and gird thyself, and serve me, till I have eaten and drunken; and afterward thou shalt eat and drink? Doth he thank the servant because he did the things that were commanded? Even so ye also, when ye shall have done all the things that are commanded you, say, We are unprofitable servants; we have done that which it was our duty to do.—Luke 17: 7-10.

Jesus often boldly took his illustrations from the facts of life even when they were repellent to him. Here he holds up the joyless life of a Syrian agricultural laborer. After plodding all day in the field, this man comes home, tired and hungry. Is he promptly cared for? No, he must first cook and serve his master's meal. Then he can eat what's left. Does he get any thanks for working overtime? Not a thank. Now, says Jesus, what this man does under the hard coercion of his lot, you and I must do of our own free will. After we have done a man's work, let us go and do some more for the sake of the cause, and disclaim praise. That spirit of utter service is, in fact, the spirit in which men work when the Kingdom vision gets hold of them. They become greedy for work and can not satisfy themselves. The strong and inspired men always feel at the end that they have not done half they ought to have done. The last words of Martin Luther, scribbled on a scrap of paper, were: "We are beggars. That's true."

What would Jesus say to a college student who is chronically tired and who feels that he is laying his professors and his father under heavy obligation by working at all?

He worked his way thru College he said and I think he told a truth

STUDY FOR THE WEEK

Is it not a strange fate that down to the most recent times art has pictured Jesus all meek and gentle, and theology has emphasized his passive suffering? Yet he was high-power energy. His epigrams and hyperboles crack like a whip-lash. He was up before dawn. He always rose to the

He worked & professors he w. his dad and he worked all his friends for—oorth—

71

sight of human need. To do the will of his Father was meat and drink to him. His life was a combat. He faced opposition without flinching and "stedfastly set his face to go up to Jerusalem" when he knew it meant death. Even when he stood silent before the court and when he hung nailed to the gallows, he was a spiritual force in action and men were disturbed and afraid before him.

I

He communicated energy to others. He hated mere talk and discouraged fruitless theorizing. He praised energetic action when he found it, as in the case of Zacchæus, and of the men who climbed the roof with a paralytic man and dug up the roofing to let him down to Jesus. He called that sort of thing "faith." Faith, in Jesus' use of the word, did not mean shutting your eyes and folding your hands. He said it was an explosive that could remove mountains. He gave three of his disciples nicknames, and they were all given to express forcefulness; Simon he called Peter, the Rock; and James and John he called Boanerges, the sons of thunder. He sent his disciples open-eyed to face trouble; he told them the wolves were waiting for them, but to rejoice and be exceeding glad for the chance of lining up against them. Let us clear our minds forever of the idea that Jesus was a mild and innocuous person who parted his hair and beard in the middle, and turned his disciples into mollycoddles. Away with it!

Though the spirit of Jesus has never had more than half a chance in historic Christianity, yet it is demonstrable that the total efficiency of humanity, the bulk of work done, and the capacity for heroic tension of energies have been greatly increased by it. Taking it on the smallest scale—every real conversion means a break with debasing habits, with alcoholism, with the waste of sexual energies; it means more self-control, more responsiveness to duty, more capacity to take a long outlook, and consequently better work. We can observe this in ourselves and others. We still need the coercion of stern necessity and of public opinion to keep us straight, but an inward compulsion is added. A Christian carries his policeman around inside of him. Where Christianity gets a really firm hold on men or women, especially if there is a basis of natural ability, it pushes them on to lead in moral movements and they break a way for human progress.

When Christianity multiplies such cases, and makes soberness, duty, and hard work the habit of entire communities, we have a social fact of first-class importance; for the human animal is naturally lazy, sluggish, and inclined to live for today. The capacity to subordinate immediate gratification for a future good is scarce; the capacity to subordinate selfish advantage to a great common and moral good is scarcer still.

We can see this force working on a larger scale on the foreign mission field where Christianity is a new social energy. There it is easier to disentangle it from other social forces. What are the comparative results when it gets a lodgment in a single social class or tribal group? This question will bear watching during the next fifty years. The full social results of Christianity will not show till the third generation.

We get another demonstration of increased working efficiency in humanity wherever Christianity has passed through an internal purification which has set free more of its spiritual energies. What, for instance, has been the historic connection between the development of capitalistic industry in Holland, England, and France, and the sober and frugal piety and patient laboriousness created in the Calvinists of Holland, the Puritans of England, and the Huguenots of France?

II

The contributions made by Christianity to the working efficiency and the constructive social abilities of humanity in the past have been mainly indirect. The main aim set before

Christians was to save their souls from eternal woe, to have communion with God now and hereafter, and to live God-fearing lives. It was individualistic religion, concentrated on the life to come. Its social effectiveness was largely a by-product. What, now, would have been the result if Christianity had placed an equally strong emphasis on the Kingdom of God, the ideal social order? Other things being equal, a Christian father and mother are better parents than others because they have more sense of duty, more love, and a higher valuation of spiritual things. But if, in addition, they have a religious desire for a higher social order and realize that noble children are a splendid contribution to it, how will that affect their parenthood? A teacher, artist, or scientist who is also a religious man, will do conscientious work if he works under the motives of individualistic religion. But if he has a vision of the Kingdom of God on earth and sees the contributions he can make to it, will not that raise the character of his output? A business man of strong Christian character will work hard, keep his word in business, and deal fairly with employes and customers. But would not a new direction be given to his moral energies if his religion taught him that he must help to shape the workings of industry and trade so that hereafter there will be no fundamental clash between business and the morals of Christianity?

What the world of Christian men and women needs is to have a great social objective set before them and laid on their conscience with the authority of religion. Then religion would get behind social evolution in earnest.

This would be no new and foreign element imported into our religion. It would be a modern revival of the doctrine of Jesus himself, which has been too long submerged and neglected. One chief reason why it was side-tracked is that no despotic State and no society dominated by a predatory class ever wanted religion applied to a reconstruction of the social order. The idea of the Kingdom of God reawoke with the rise of modern democracy. Now is the time for it.

III

The idea of the Kingdom of God is not identified with any special social theory. It means justice, freedom, fraternity, labor, joy. Let each social system and movement show us what it can contribute and we will weigh its claims. We want the old ideal defined in modern terms, in the terms of modern democracy, of the power machine, of international peace, and of evolutionary science. But we want to embrace it with the old religious faith and ardor, so that we can pray over it.

This great task of establishing a righteous social life on earth embraces all minor tasks in so far as they are good. The mother who tries to make a good home, the farmer who feeds the people, the teacher who trains them, the scientist who gets the facts for all, the merchant, the workingman, the artist, the leader in play—they are all contributing to the Kingdom, provided they view their work so, and are trying to put an evolutionary *plus* into it which will lift the total nearer to the divine will. The Kingdom is the supreme task, and all small tasks are part of it. That gives every man a place in it who works—where is the idler's place in it?—and it hallows all good work with religious glory.

It may seem as if this social aim of religion may depreciate the aim of developing our own personality and of saving our souls. It ought not. Sometimes it does for a time. But we are each so enormously important to ourselves that we are not likely to forget ourselves, and the practical struggle with temptation and sorrow will teach us to seek strength for our personal needs from Christ. In time we shall learn to say with Jesus, "For their sakes I sanctify myself, that they also may be sanctified." In time surrender to the Kingdom ideal, toil for it, self-denial for it, cooperation with others for it, will have the strongest kind of reactions on ourselves and our moral fiber. Gymnasium work is all right, but real work in the open is better. We are most durably saved by putting in hard work for the Kingdom of God.

In every great task a religious man is consciously thrown back on the aid of God—most of all in the greatest task of all. Eternal powers are cooperating with our puny efforts. That alone guarantees that our work is not wasted. We plant and water, but unless God's sun shines upon it, our work is nothing. He is a fool that is not reverent and humble. We sorely need this faith in the collaboration and patience of God today when so much of the best spiritual achievement of mankind is swept away, and we seem far away from a kingdom of love. "As the heavens are higher than the earth, so are my ways higher than your ways, and my thoughts than your thoughts."

IV

Here, then, we have another social principle of Jesus. A collective moral ideal is a necessity for the individual and the race. Every man must have a conscious determination to help in his own place to work out a righteous social order for and with God. The race must increasingly turn its own evolution into a conscious process. It owes that duty to itself and to God who seeks an habitation in it. It must seek to realize its divine destiny. "Thy kingdom come! Thy will be done on earth as it is done in heaven!" This is the conscious evolutionary program of Jesus. It combines religion, social science, and ethical action in a perfect synthesis.

What has this to say to students? Everything, it seems.

First, whatever is to be our particular job, we must relate it to the supreme common task at which God and all good men are working. Unless we see and assert that relation, we are mere day-laborers or slaves, with neither intelligence nor enthusiasm.

Second, anyone who, instead of loyally relating his life-work to God's work, pursues his own ambition at the expense of the Kingdom and damages it to make profit for himself, is like a man who takes pay to damage his country. He makes the work harder for all who are more faithful than he, and their blood will be upon him.

Third, *"noblesse oblige."* If we belong to the republic of learning and education, something extra is justly due from us. Here, for instance, is the evangelization of the world in this generation. An organization has been created to accomplish it. Heroic pioneers have died, preparing the way for larger forces. Is our life fit and good enough to put into that? Here is the Christianization of the social order in the next two generations. What have all our social studies been for in the design of God? To fit ourselves for exploiting our fellows or to show them the way to the Kingdom of God?

SUGGESTIONS FOR THOUGHT AND DISCUSSION

I. *Our Untapped Reserves*

1. How far is a person who produces nothing, of use to the community? Is increase of productive efficiency the test of progress?

2. Does religion help to call out reserves of energy in human nature?

II. *The Energy of Jesus*

1. How far did Jesus give evidence of audacity and high power energy? Has the Christian Church realized this? How about the portrayals of him in art?

2. Furnish evidence that Jesus demanded sincere work. How was this connected with the Kingdom of God in his mind?

3. Give proof that he demanded heroism of his followers as a commonplace thing.

4. How did this temper affect his view of prayer?

III. *Christianity and Work*

1. Has Christianity ever promoted idleness? If so, what type of Christianity was it?

2. Taken as a whole has Christianity increased the amount of work done, or lessened it? Give historical proof.

3. Would it raise the economic efficiency of an African tribe to become Christians? Would it raise the efficiency of the Mexican people if they adopted a purer type of Christianity? How?

4. Where is the idler's place in the Kingdom of God?

IV. *The Reenforcement of Christianity by the Kingdom Ideal*

1. Is a call to be converted a call to enjoy spiritual peace or to exert spiritual energy?

2. How has the idea arisen that Christianity is a "dope" to make people contented amid wrong conditions?

3. How would the Kingdom faith give religious quality to the plain man's job?

4. Other things being equal, has a religious man more or less fighting energy against wrong than a non-religious man?

5. If a man passes from an individualistic to a social conception of religion, what change will it make in moral action?

6. To what extent is the enterprise of the Kingdom of God a dynamic expression of accepted sociological principles?

7. What is the special obligation of college men and women to the Kingdom of God?

V. *For Special Discussion*

1. Is the Kingdom of God to be brought about by an act of God in the future or by the work of men in the present? Does the one exclude the other?

2. Does our social order call out the full energy and intelligence of the working people?

3. Can an overworked and underpaid workman feel that he is working for the Kingdom of God?

4. Does the Kingdom of God necessarily involve elements of social readjustment and change?

5. Would a predatory governing class in the past have allowed the preaching of a social conception of the Kingdom of God?

12-10

CHAPTER VI

A NEW AGE AND NEW STANDARDS

As the Kingdom Comes Ethical Standards Must Advance

Every approximation to the Reign of God in humanity demands an advance in the social relations of men, that is, an advance in ethics. Every really epochal advance must have it or slip back. There must be, first, better obedience to the moral principles already recognized and accepted by society; second, an expansion of the sway of ethical duty to new fields and wider groups of humanity; and third, a recognition of new duties and the assimilation of new and higher ethical conceptions.

To what extent did Jesus appreciate these supreme needs?

DAILY READINGS

FIRST DAY: *Living up to the Old Standards*

In the high-priesthood of Annas and Caiaphas, the word of God came unto John the son of Zacharias in the wilderness. And he came into all the region round about the Jordan, preaching the baptism of repentance unto remission of sins; as it is written in the book of the words of Isaiah the prophet,

The voice of one crying in the wilderness,
Make ye ready the way of the Lord,
Make his paths straight.
Every valley shall be filled,
And every mountain and hill shall be brought low;
And the crooked shall become straight,
And the rough ways smooth;
And all flesh shall see the salvation of God.

He said therefore to the multitudes that went out to be baptized of him, Ye offspring of vipers, who warned you to flee from the wrath to come? Bring forth therefore fruits worthy of repentance, and begin not to say within yourselves, We have Abraham to our father: for I say unto you, that God is able of these stones to raise up children unto Abraham. And even now the axe also lieth at the root of the trees: every tree therefore that bringeth not forth good fruit is hewn down, and cast into the fire. —Luke 3: 2-9.

The ABC of social renewal and moral advance is for each of us to face our sins sincerely and get on a basis of frankness with God and ourselves. Therefore Christianity set out with a call for personal repentance. If we only acted up to what we know to be right, this world would be a different place. But we fool ourselves with protective coloring devices in order to keep our own self-respect. Take our language, for instance; it reeks with evasive euphemisms intended to make nasty sins look prettier. We call stealing "swiping" and cheating "cribbing." When we have been drunk we say we were "squiffy." As soon as we face the facts, we realize that what we call peccadilloes in ourselves are the black sins that have slain the innocents and have hag ridden humanity through all its history. That is the beginning of social vision. Personal repentance is a social advance.

What equivalent have college men and women for the plea of the Pharisees that they were Abraham's children and had a pull with God?

SECOND DAY: *Expanding the Area of Obligation*

And behold, a certain lawyer stood up and made trial of him, saying, Teacher, what shall I do to inherit eternal life? And he said unto him, What is written in the law? how readest thou? And he answering said, Thou shalt love the Lord thy God with all thy heart, and with all thy soul, and with all thy strength, and with all thy mind; and thy neighbor as thyself. And he said unto him, Thou hast answered right: this do, and thou shalt live. But he, desiring to justify himself, said unto Jesus, And who is my neighbor? Jesus made answer and said, A certain man was going down from Jerusalem to Jericho; and he fell among robbers, who both stripped him and beat him, and departed, leaving him half dead. And by chance a certain priest was going down that way: and when he saw him, he passed by on the other side. And in like manner a Levite also, when he came to the place, and saw him, passed by on the other side. But a certain Samaritan, as he journeyed, came where he was: and when he saw him, he was moved with compassion, and came to him, and bound up his wounds, pouring on them oil and wine; and he set him on his own beast, and brought him to an inn, and took care of him. And on the morrow he took out two shillings, and gave them to the host, and said, Take care of him; and whatsoever thou spendest more, I, when I come back again, will repay thee. Which of these three, thinkest thou, proved neighbor unto him that fell among the robbers? And he said, He that showed mercy on him. And Jesus said unto him, Go, and do thou likewise.—Luke 10: 25-37.

A meaty story and a famous one. The lawyer found his own answer uncomfortably simple when it was taken up in such a matter-of-fact way. It was suddenly up to him to act on his own advice. He tried to hedge by raising a new question: "Love my neighbor? Certainly. But who is my neighbor?" Who is within the cordon of fraternal fellowship with me? All men of my people and religion? Or only the good and desirable people? Where do you draw the line? Follows the story of the Good Samaritan. "Your neighbor? The alien and the heretic." The logic of the reply demanded that some good Jew would be shown caring for a wounded Samaritan. Jesus gives it a smashing effectiveness by reversing the role and showing the hated Samaritan as the heroic lover of his kind. To get the situation we must remember the historic enmity between the Jews and the half-breed aliens who had stolen their land and their religion while they were exiled. If we substitute Spaniard and Moor, Kurd and Armenian, Serb and Bulgar, we may get the tension.

Who are our American Samaritans? "Sir Americans"
12-15-19

THIRD DAY: *Raising the Standards*

We must live up to what we know is right, and we must expand the area of ethical obligation to take in even men of alien race and hostile religion. But beyond that, we need a conscious advance in the ethical standards themselves. Jesus worked out this principle with perfect clearness in a part of the Sermon on the Mount, Matthew 5: 17-48. He states the need, and then shows in six cases how such an advance would work out. We shall take these up in their order. Matthew has introduced scattered sayings of Jesus which serve as corollaries, but which do not bear directly on the real course of the argument; for instance, Matthew 5: 23-26; 29-30. In our quotations in this and the following days we shall confine ourselves to the main line of thought in order to concentrate attention on that.

> Think not that I came to destroy the law or the prophets: I came not to destroy, but to fulfil. . . .
> For I say unto you, that except your righteousness shall exceed the righteousness of the scribes and Pharisees, ye shall in no wise enter into the kingdom of heaven.—Matt. 5: 17, 20.

Apparently conservative Jews soon felt the spiritual freedom and force in the teachings of Jesus. He seemed to them to be attacking the sacred Law, the foundation of morality and religion. Jesus mentions the charge but denies it. His purpose was not destructive but constructive. He demanded not less righteousness but more. The lines of right living needed to be prolonged. The traditional standards were no longer adequate. A man might obey them and yet not be a good man. The scribes and Pharisees were the model church members of Judaism and experts in piety, yet they were not qualified to enter the Kingdom of God.

Are we also good people who are not good enough?

Do Something ~ Be

FOURTH DAY: *The Sins of Hate*

> Ye have heard that it was said to them of old time, Thou shalt not kill; and whosoever shall kill shall be in danger of the judgment: but I say unto you, that every one who is angry with his brother shall be in danger of the judgment; and whosoever shall say to his brother, Raca, shall be in danger of the council; and whosoever shall say, Thou fool, shall be in danger of the hell of fire.—Matt. 5: 21, 22.

The Law of Moses forbade murder; a man-slayer was amenable in the ordinary court. Was this an adequate expression of the sacredness of human life and personality? It never even scratched a man or woman who assaulted the soul of another with anger and curses. Jesus proposed that these sins be restandardized. Plain anger ought to be valued about as murder used to be. And if anybody went so far as to revile a brother and deny his moral or intellectual worth, the Supreme Court and Gehenna would be about right for him. The lawyers' gauge of culpability can not get down to the subtler expressions of lovelessness which break the prime law of the Kingdom.

By what methods is contempt expressed in our own social life?
How highly do we rate the moral value of self-respect?

FIFTH DAY: *The Sins of Sex*

> Ye have heard that it was said, Thou shalt not

commit adultery: but I say unto you, that every one
that looketh on a woman to lust after her hath com-
mitted adultery with her already in his heart. . . .

It was said also, Whosoever shall put away his
wife, let him give here a writing of divorcement:
but I say unto you, that every one that putteth away
his wife, saving for the cause of fornication, maketh
her an adulteress; and whosoever shall marry her
when she is put away committeth adultery.—Matt.
5: 27, 28; 31, 32.

These two cases deal with sex. The old law forbade
adultery, the infringement of family life, and stopped there.
Jesus goes back of the act to the lustful imaginations and
the wandering eye, which may lack opportunity but which
are the real spring of all uncleanness. He runs the line of
ethical obligation farther back.

The law of divorce (Deut. 24: 1), especially as interpreted by the scribes, was very comfortable—for the male.
He could divorce his wife for almost any cause. Her only
protection was that a formal paper had to be given her
which enabled her to marry again. As a woman's economic
and social standing in that age depended almost wholly on
her family relations, she was at the mercy of the man. Jesus
demanded more protection for her. To him the relation was
indissoluble. The Mosaic provision for divorce was a con-
cession to the low moral level of the people. The ideal was
the "one man, one woman" provision of the Creator. (See
Matt. 19: 3-8). The disciples ruefully remarked that such
a strengthening of the bond did not add to the attractiveness of marriage—for the male (19: 10).

Where do we draw the line between the rightful, natural
desire of sex and lawless predatory lust?

SIXTH DAY: *The Sins of Words*

Again, ye have heard that it was said to them of
old time, Thou shalt not forswear thyself, but shalt

perform unto the Lord thine oaths: but I say unto
you, Swear not at all; neither by the heaven, for it
is the throne of God; nor by the earth, for it is the
footstool of his feet; nor by Jerusalem, for it is the
city of the great King. Neither shalt thou swear by
thy head, for thou canst not make one hair white or
black. But let your speech be, Yea, yea; Nay, nay:
and whatsoever is more than these is of the evil one.
—Matt. 5: 33-37.

Current morality had reached the point of insisting on
truthfulness when a man was under oath. Solemnly to call
God to witness a statement and yet to fool your neighbor by
it, was downright wicked. But it was very handy. So they
developed a joyful lot of casuistical distinctions as to which
kind of oaths were binding and which didn't count. See how
Jesus ridiculed this (Matt. 23: 16-22). Here he proposed that
the obligation of veracity be extended to all statements. A
truthful man needs no oaths to assure a doubting world that
this time he is really telling what is so. Oaths are a device
of the devil to limit the amount of truth in the world.

How about oaths for legal purposes? Could they be dis-
pensed with? Have they done more good or harm?

SEVENTH DAY: *The Sins of Strife*

Ye have heard that it was said, An eye for an eye,
and a tooth for a tooth: but I say unto you, Resist
not him that is evil: but whosoever smiteth thee on
thy right cheek, turn to him the other also. And if
any man would go to law with thee, and take away
thy coat, let him have thy cloak also. And whosoever shall compel thee to go one mile, go with him
two. Give to him that asketh thee, and from him
that would borrow of thee turn not thou away.
Ye have heard that it was said, Thou shalt love
thy neighbor, and hate thine enemy: but I say unto
you, Love your enemies, and pray for them that persecute you; that ye may be sons of your Father who

is in heaven: for he maketh his sun to rise on the
evil and the good, and sendeth rain on the just and
the unjust. For if ye love them that love you, what
reward have ye? do not even the publicans the same?
And if ye salute your brethren only, what do ye
more than others? do not even the Gentiles the same?
Ye therefore shall be perfect, as your heavenly Father
is perfect.—Matt. 5: 38-48.

The Law restricted the natural desire for revenge to the
limit of a strict equivalent. If a man knocked out your tooth,
you could knock out one for him, but not two teeth, nor
all he had. Of course retaliation never heals a feud. Jesus
proposes to limit revenge still farther and to retaliate only
by acts of kindness. That is, in fact, the only way to end
a quarrel completely and victoriously. It reestablishes fellowship and kills an enemy.

The Law called for love for one's neighbors; the scribes
had added the permission to hate one's enemies. Jesus raises
the standards of good-will. The law of love applies to all.
There is nothing great in loving those who love us. Anybody can do that. Heroic love begins where no love comes
to meet it. Those who can win that triumph show the true
family likeness of God, and are now living in his Kingdom.

*What are our personal experiences as to the utility of
revenge?*

*What is the difference between the non-resistance which
Jesus proposed, and cowardice?*

Is there such a thing in fact as loving your enemies?

Study for the Week

I

The Hebrew religion was an unfinished religion. That is
one of the best proofs of its divine inspiration. The prophets
had the forward look. Great things were yet to come. As
one of the most daring expressed it, the old and hallowed

covenant, made by God at the Exodus, would be superseded by a new and higher relation; God would write his
law into the hearts of the people; the old drill in outward
statutes would disappear, for all men would know God by
an inward experience of forgiveness and love (Jeremiah 31:
31-34).

Jesus not only shared this expectation of a new religious
era, but set it in the center of his teaching. Religion to him
was not static. He lived in a moving world. A new age
was coming, and he would be the initiator of it. "From the
days of John the Baptist until now the kingdom of God suf-
fereth violence, and men of violence take it by force." John
had been the greatest of the prophets; with him a new swift
movement had begun; but something far greater was coming; even the least in the new age would have an advantage
over John (Matt. 11: 11-19).

The popular conception expected the new age to come by
divine miraculous interference simply. The Messiah would
descend from heaven with angelic legions, expel the Romans,
judge the nation, punish the apostate Jews, and then the
new Jerusalem, which was already complete and waiting in
heaven, would descend from above. That was the Utopia
of Jewish apocalypticism. Jesus never eliminated the direct
acts of God and the significance of divine catastrophes from
his outlook. But in his parables taken from biological proc-
esses (see especially Matthew 13) he developed a conception of continuous and quiet growth, culminating at last in
the judgment act of God. The Kingdom of God, he said,
is like a farmer who sows his grain and lets the forces of
nature work; he goes about his daily tasks, and all the time
the tiny blades come up, the ear forms and gets heavy, and
then comes the harvest (Mark 4: 26-29). Jesus was working his way toward evolutionary conceptions. They were so
new to his followers that he put them in parable form to
avoid antagonism.

Such a conception of the Kingdom brought it closer to
human action. It was already at work; it was in one sense

already present (Luke 17: 20-21). It was possible then to help it along.

The most obvious duty was for every man to clean up his own backyard and repent of his sins. Every one should approximate the life of the Kingdom by living now as he would expect to live then. But, as we have seen from his sayings, Jesus went far beyond this. He demanded an elevation of the accepted ethical standards. It was not simply a matter of erring and lagging individuals, but of the socialized norms of conduct. He had deep reverence and loyalty for the religion of his nation, and never told his followers to break with it. But he asserted boldly that the customary ethics of Judaism, based on the Decalogue and its interpretation by the Jewish theologians, was not good enough. It was good as far as it went, and he had no destructive criticism of it, but it needed to be "fulfilled" and to have its lines prolonged.

We have studied the six sample instances which he offered in order to explain his principle of moral and social progress. In each case he accepts the law as it stood, but asks for more of the same thing, more respect for personality, more reverence for womanhood, more stability for the home, more truthfulness, more peacefulness, more love. Thus he combined continuity with progress, conservatism with radicalism.

II

The platform for ethical progress laid down in the Sermon on the Mount is a great platform. When Tolstoi first realized the social significance of these simple sentences, it acted as a revelation which changed his life. Even men who reject the supernatural claims of Christianity uncover before the Sermon on the Mount. Yet its fate is tragic. It has not been "damned with faint praise," but made ineffective by universal praise. Its commandments are lifted so high that nobody feels under obligations to act on them. Only small sections of the Christian Church have taken the sayings on oaths, non-resistance, and love of enemies to mean what they say and to be obligatory. Yet all feel that the line of ethical and social advance must lie in the direction traced by Jesus, and if society could only climb out of the present pit of predatory selfishness and meanness to that level, it would be heaven.

Do you and I believe in it? Do we believe that it is not enough to keep out of the spiritual hell and damnation of adultery, but that a clean mind would be the most efficient and cheerful mind? Do we believe that a man who forgives and keeps sweet is happier and safer than a man who always resents things and stirs the witches' caldron of hate in his soul? If a man loved his enemy and turned the other cheek, would he be everybody's door-mat or everybody's temple of refuge?

Suppose we mark for the present those parts which we are willing to accept as our own standards of action. If there are portions which do not seem practicable, let us post them in our minds as debatable propositions, as points to be tested by the experience of coming years, or as working hypotheses in the science of living.

But whatever we may think of single points, let us stick to the leading thought of Jesus, that every advance toward the Kingdom of God, that is, toward the true social order, involves a raising of the ethical standards accepted by society. This is a principle of social progress which every leading intellect ought to know by heart.

III

When Jesus offered his six sample cases of ethical progress, he had no intention of exhausting the principle of advance which he laid down. There was more to say about the Jewish law. It is now for his followers to treat the inherited ethical conceptions of traditional Christianity with the same combination of reverence and courage with which he treated the Jewish law.

From the beginning Christianity taught self-control and the mastery of the spirit over physical desires. It always condemned drunkenness. But ancient Christianity never demanded abstinence from fermented drink. With modern methods of manufacturing alcoholic drinks and modern capitalistic methods of pushing their sale, the danger has become more pressing. With modern scientific knowledge the physiological and social problems of drink have become clearer. Modern life demands an undrugged nervous system for quick and steady reactions. It was said of old time, "Thou shalt not get drunk"; but today the spirit of Christianity and modern life says, "Thou shalt not drink nor sell intoxicants at all."

In every case in which the interests of woman came before Jesus, he took her side. At that time woman was the suppressed half of humanity. The attitude of historic Christianity has been a mixture between his spirit and the spirit of the patriarchal family. Today Christianity is plainly prolonging the line of respect and spiritual valuation to the point of equality between men and women—and beyond.

From the beginning an emancipating force resided in Christianity which was bound to register its effects in political life. But in an age of despotism it might have to confine its political morality to the duty of patient submission, and content itself with offering little sanctuaries of freedom to the oppressed in the Christian fraternities. Today, in the age of democracy, it has become immoral to endure private ownership of government. It is no longer a sufficient righteousness to live a good life in private. Christianity needs an ethic of public life.

It was said of old "Thou shalt not commit murder." It is said to us, "Ye shall not wear down life in the young by premature hard labor; nor let the fear of poverty freeze the fountain of life; and ye shall put a stop to war."

It was said of old, "Thou shalt not steal." It is said to us, "Ye shall take no unearned gain from your fellows, but pay to society in productive labor what ye take from it in goods."

IV

This matter of raising the moral standards of society is preeminently an affair of the young. They must do it or it will never be done. The Sermon on the Mount was spoken by a young man, and it moves with the impetuous virility of youth. The old are water-logged physically. They are mentally bound up with the institutions inside of which they have spent a lifetime, and they want to enjoy in peace the wealth and position they have attained. We shall be just the same forty years from now. But while we are young is the time to make a forward run with the flag of Christ, the banner of justice and love, and plant it on the heights yonder. We must not only be better men and women than we are now. We must leave a better world behind us when we are through with it. Whatever we affirm in our growing years will work out in some fashion in our years of maturity and power. If fifty thousand college men and women a year would range themselves alongside of Jesus Christ, look at our present world as open-eyed as he looked at his world, see where the social standards of conduct are in contradiction with his spirit and with modern need, and work to raise them, the world would feel the effect in ten years. And those who would strive in that way would live by faith in the higher commonwealth of God and have some of its nobility of spirit.

SUGGESTIONS FOR THOUGHT AND DISCUSSION

I. *Living Up to the Old Standards*

1. What would happen if a college community began to live up to the standards of work and honor which all acknowledge?

2. Does human nature welcome a moral advance?

II. *The Ethical Program of Jesus*

1. What advance does Jesus' program make necessary? State the main principle in Matt. 5:17-48, and the six appli-

cations made by Jesus himself. How was this principle connected with his idea of the Kingdom?

2. Can we agree with the principle? How far can we go with Jesus in his application?

3. Would a man get more or less satisfaction out of life if he obeyed these maxims in private life?

4. How far could a man hold his own if he obeyed them in a reasonable way in business or in public life? If a man loved his enemies and turned the other cheek, would he be everybody's doormat or everybody's friend and refuge?

III. *Raising the Standards Today*

1. On what ethical questions have we come to the point where the moral standards accepted by society can be and must be raised?

2. If you could purchase one single advance by your life, what would you choose?

3. How does an expansion of the area of full social obligation operate to raise the standards of conduct? Who is my neighbor, and who is not?

IV. *For Special Discussion*

1. A new intellectual age has opened with the rise of modern science; what new moral standards should be the result of our new knowledge?

2. A new economic age opened with the invention of power machinery and the social organization of labor; what new moral standards should have been the result of the new wealth of civilization?

3. A new political era opened with the rise of democracy; what new moral standards should be achieved in the life of States and cities?

4. A new era began in world-wide relations with the beginning of steam-carried commerce; what new standards are needed for international and inter-racial relations?

PART III

THE RECALCITRANT SOCIAL FORCES

CHAPTER VII

LEADERSHIP FOR SERVICE

Ambition Must Get Its Satisfaction by Serving Humanity

The Kingdom of God was an ideal. If it was to be turned into concrete realities, it would encounter the recalcitrant and stubborn instincts of human nature and the conservative forces of society. Where did Jesus locate the obstacles? At what points was he aware of resistance? Did he realize the force of ambition and the love of power? Did he gauge the pull of the property instinct? Did he feel religion as a help or a hindrance in realizing the Kingdom of God? These questions we shall follow up in three lessons.

DAILY READINGS

FIRST DAY: *The Trustee*

"Father was right" nunney, Dec 19 Jan 20

And Peter said, Lord, speakest thou this parable unto us, or even unto all? And the Lord said, Who then is the faithful and wise steward, whom his lord shall set over his household, to give them their portion of food in due season? Blessed is that servant, whom his lord when he cometh shall find so doing. Of a truth I say unto you, that he will set him over all that he hath. But if that servant shall say in his heart, My lord delayeth his coming; and shall begin to beat the menservants and the maidservants, and to eat and drink, and to be drunken; the lord of that servant shall come in a day when he expecteth not, and in an hour when he knoweth not, and shall cut him asunder, and appoint his por-

97

tion with the unfaithful. And that servant, who knew his lord's will, and made not ready, nor did according to his will, shall be beaten with many stripes; but he that knew not, and did things worthy of stripes, shall be beaten with few stripes. And to whomsoever much is given, of him shall much be required: and to whom they commit much, of him will they ask the more.—Luke 12: 41-48.

The preceding verses (v. 35-40) dealt with the faithfulness of the rank and file; this parable deals with the responsibility of official position and sketches the alternative of selfish and serviceable leadership. The head steward had charge of a great estate, directing the labor of workmen and maids, dealing out supplies, and controlling the welfare and happiness of all. The absence of the master made his authority for the time absolute. Would he use it for the good of all? If so, wider scope and higher honor would come to him. Or would he become intoxicated with power, take things easy, boss his fellow-servants around, and become a petty tyrant? If so, he would get what was coming to him. Every man's duty is measured by his knowledge and by his power. If, therefore, a man rises to leadership, and finds his elbow-room enlarging, let him stiffen his sense of duty to correspond, or there will be trouble. Degeneration by power is written all over history.

The functions of a head steward belong to the age of great landowners. How would you modernize this parable to express the same ideas?

SECOND DAY: *Preparing for the Use of Power*

Then was Jesus led up of the Spirit into the wilderness to be tempted of the devil. And when he had fasted forty days and forty nights, he afterward hungered. And the tempter came and said unto him, If thou art the Son of God, command that these stones become bread. But he answered and said, It is written, Man shall not live by bread alone, but by every word that proceedeth out of the mouth of God. Then the devil taketh him into the holy city; and he set him on the pinnacle of the temple, and saith unto him, If thou art the Son of God, cast thyself down: for it is written,

He shall give his angels charge concerning thee: and,

On their hands they shall bear thee up,

Lest haply thou dash thy foot against a stone.

Jesus said unto him, Again it is written, Thou shalt not make trial of the Lord thy God. Again, the devil taketh him unto an exceeding high mountain, and showeth him all the kingdoms of the world, and the glory of them; and he said unto him, All these things will I give thee, if thou wilt fall down and worship me. Then saith Jesus unto him, Get thee hence, Satan: for it is written, Thou shalt worship the Lord thy God, and him only shalt thou serve.—Matt. 4: 1-10.

The baptism of Jesus was an act of dedication to the coming reign of God, and it brought him a deep spiritual experience. He came out of it with the sense of an immediate mission, of being called to a supreme leadership, and with the consciousness of power to correspond with his destiny. At once he confronted the question: How would he employ his Messianic power? By what means would he obtain leadership? In the desert his mind was concentrated on these problems. This story displays the temptations of a leader, and sums up his settlement on three points: first, he realized that he must not swerve aside for personal gratification, but must serve the will of God only; second, he must not debase his power by playing for popularity by means of spectacular, miraculous display; third, he must not win his leadership by methods that would mortgage him to the prince of this world, for instance by the use of force.

How would these points apply to a young man seeking political office, intellectual eminence, or artistic achievement?

Have we ever had a time of religious concentration to consider the problems of our future leadership?

THIRD DAY: *The New Principle of Leadership*

Then came to him the mother of the sons of Zebedee with her sons, worshipping him, and asking a certain thing of him. And he said unto her, What wouldest thou? She saith unto him, Command that these my two sons may sit, one on thy right hand, and one on thy left hand, in thy kingdom. But Jesus answered and said, Ye know not what ye ask. Are ye able to drink the cup that I am about to drink? They say unto him, We are able. He saith unto them, My cup indeed ye shall drink: but to sit on my right hand, and on my left hand, is not mine to give; but it is for them for whom it hath been prepared of my Father. And when the ten heard it, they were moved with indignation concerning the two brethren. But Jesus called them unto him, and said, Ye know that the rulers of the Gentiles lord it over them, and their great ones exercise authority over them. Not so shall it be among you: but whosoever would become great among you shall be your minister; and whosoever would be first among you shall be your servant: even as the Son of man came not to be ministered unto, but to minister, and to give his life a ransom for many.—Matt. 20: 20-28.

This passage is fundamental for our subject. It is the clearest formulation of the social principle involved in leadership. It contrasts two opposite types of leadership throughout human history. Salome and her sons thought Jesus was going to Jerusalem to inaugurate his Kingdom. They asked for an advance pledge assuring them of the chief place. Jesus replied that that place would not go by favoritism. There is a price to be paid for leadership in his reign, and God alone will allot the final honors. He felt in their request a relapse into conceptions that he detested. In all political organizations he saw the tyrannical use of power over the people. There must be an end of that in the new social order. Ambition must seek its satisfaction by distinguished service, and only extra-hazardous service shall win honor. He himself proposed to be a leader of that new type, and to give his life as a ransom for the emancipation of the people.

Our Master here offers each of us the conscious choice between two principles of action. *Have we made our choice?*
He offers a norm for estimating the real value of men in public life. *Have we ever tried to apply it?*

FOURTH DAY: *The History of a Governing Class*

Hear another parable: There was a man that was a householder, who planted a vineyard, and set a hedge about it, and digged a winepress in it, and built a tower, and let it out to husbandmen, and went into another country. And when the season of the fruits drew near, he sent his servants to the husbandmen, to receive his fruits. And the husbandmen took his servants, and beat one, and killed another, and stoned another. Again, he sent other servants more than the first: and they did unto them in like manner. But afterward he sent unto them his son, saying, They will reverence my son. But the husbandmen, when they saw the son, said among themselves, This is the heir; come, let us kill him, and take his inheritance. And they took him, and cast him forth out of the vineyard, and killed him. When therefore the lord of the vineyard shall come, what will he do unto those husbandmen? They say unto him, He will miserably destroy those miserable men, and will let out the vineyard unto other husbandmen, who shall render him the fruits in their seasons. Jesus saith unto them, Did ye never read in the scriptures,

The stone which the builders rejected,
The same was made the head of the corner;
This was from the Lord,

And it is marvellous in our eyes? Therefore say I unto you, The kingdom of God shall be taken

> away from you, and shall be given to a nation bring-
> ing forth the fruits thereof. And he that falleth on
> this stone shall be broken to pieces: but on whom-
> soever it shall fall, it will scatter him as dust. And
> when the chief priests and the Pharisees heard his
> parables, they perceived that he spake of them. And
> when they sought to lay hold on him, they feared
> the multitudes, because they took him for a prophet.
> —Matt. 21: 33-46.

A delegation of the chief priests, lawyers, and elders challenged the authority of Jesus to act as he did. He replied
by challenging their authority to act as they did. The vineyard parable sums up his view of the moral history of the
governing class in his nation. It was like a group of men
who had rented a vineyard on shares, but took advantage of
the owner's absence to embezzle his share, insolently to beat
up his representatives, and to put themselves in possession
of the farm. Every demand of God for righteousness in the
history of Israel had been resisted by those in power. What
title, then, did they have to the rights they claimed? Unless
they fulfilled the function of true leaders, why should they
not be put out of power and brought to justice? In this
passage, then, we have a characterization of leaders who take
the profits and honors of leadership, without performing its
higher duties to God and humanity.

Is there any connection between this challenge of Jesus,
and the functional theories of society and the evolutionary
conception of history?

FIFTH DAY: *An Indictment of a Governing Class*

> Then spake Jesus to the multitudes and to his dis-
> ciples, saying, The scribes and the Pharisees sit on
> Moses' seat: all things therefore whatsoever they
> bid you, these do and observe: but do not ye after
> their works; for they say, and do not. Yea, they
> bind heavy burdens and grievous to be borne, and
> lay them on men's shoulders; but they themselves

will not move them with their finger. But all their works they do to be seen of men: for they make broad their phylacteries, and enlarge the borders of their garments, and love the chief place at feasts, and the chief seats in the synagogues, and the salutations in the marketplaces, and to be called of men, Rabbi. But be not ye called Rabbi: for one is your teacher, and all ye are brethren. And call no man your father on the earth: for one is your Father, even he who is in heaven. Neither be ye called masters: for one is your master, even the Christ. But he that is greatest among you shall be your servant. And whosoever shall exalt himself shall be humbled; and whosoever shall humble himself shall be exalted.

But woe unto you, scribes and Pharisees, hypocrites! because ye shut the kingdom of heaven against men: for ye enter not in yourselves, neither suffer ye them that are entering in to enter.—Matt. 23: 1-13.

The invective against the scribes and Pharisees (Matt. 23) is a characterization of selfish leadership in the field of religion. Its fundamental elements have remained the same in all religions and through all history: fine talk and little action; religion turned into a law and a burden, in order to hold the people in obedience to the interests of the leaders; pride and ambition exploiting religion to get honors. Jesus tells the people to revolt against the titles in which this domination had found decorative satisfaction. He demands democracy, humility, brotherliness.

Does this description justly apply to the Christian ministry today, or has there been a great historical change by which that profession has become a profession of service?

Where in modern social life would the invective of Jesus against selfish leadership still be true?

Sixth Day: *The Lost Leader*

And in these days Peter stood up in the midst of

the brethren, and said (and there was a multitude of persons gathered together, about a hundred and twenty), Brethren, it was needful that the scripture should be fulfilled, which the Holy Spirit spake before by the mouth of David concerning Judas, who was guide to them that took Jesus. For he was numbered among us, and received his portion in this ministry. (Now this man obtained a field with the reward of his iniquity; and falling headlong, he burst asunder in the midst, and all his bowels gushed out. And it became known to all the dwellers at Jerusalem; insomuch that in their language that field was called Akeldama, that is, The field of blood.) For it is written in the book of Psalms,

Let his habitation be made desolate,
And let no man dwell therein:
and,
His office let another take.—Acts 1: 15-20.

The character and motives of Judas remain an unsolved riddle. The Gospels leave no doubt that money played a part with him. But could a man whom Jesus selected and trusted be actuated by so sordid a motive alone? Was he perhaps embittered because he had staked his ambition on the Galilean Messiah and Jesus failed to act the part assigned to him? Was he hoping to force him to revolutionary action? We may be sure that Judas was no slinking thief only. In Rubens' picture of the Last Supper at Milano Judas has a strong and noble face, but troubled and restless eyes, telling of a hurt soul. The other disciples were deeply impressed by his betrayal of the Master and of the common cause. Judas is the type of the lost leader. "Just for a handful of silver he left us, just for a ribbon to stick in his coat." Some leaders blunder and learn better; some sag to lower levels but plod on; some sell out. Judas could not bear to live. Read James Russell Lowell's "Extreme Unction."

Have you known of cases today of men who have abandoned or betrayed a cause to get office or income? Any who abandon humanity itself to get thirty pieces for themselves?

SEVENTH DAY: *The New Order of Leaders*

> And Jesus went about all the cities and the villages, teaching in their synagogues, and preaching the gospel of the kingdom, and healing all manner of disease and all manner of sickness. But when he saw the multitudes, he was moved with compassion for them, because they were distressed and scattered, as sheep not having a shepherd. Then saith he unto his disciples, The harvest indeed is plenteous, but the laborers are few. Pray ye therefore the Lord of the harvest, that he send forth laborers into his harvest.
>
> And he called unto him his twelve disciples, and gave them authority over unclean spirits, to cast them out, and to heal all manner of disease and all manner of sickness.
>
> Now the names of the twelve apostles are these: The first, Simon, who is called Peter, and Andrew his brother; James the son of Zebedee, and John his brother; Philip, and Bartholomew; Thomas, and Matthew the publican; James the son of Alphæus, and Thaddæus; Simon the Cananæan, and Judas Iscariot, who also betrayed him.—Matt. 9: 35–10: 4.

We have studied part of this passage before as an expression of the social feeling of Jesus. Note now that it was their leaderless condition which impressed him. Plenty of priests, lawyers, and experts on the Bible, but no friendly shepherds for the people. When he created the apostolate, he initiated a new order of leadership, a band of men who would serve and not exploit. Read the instructions he gave them (Chap. 10), and see how carefully he fences out selfish gain. Service versus exploitation, that is one of the tests of all who claim leadership in his name. We realize that in the field of religion. But why should not the same test be made in professional, political, and business life? Predatory action may not be as glaringly shameful there, but is it any the more moral?

Now what about you and me?

STUDY FOR THE WEEK

I

The desire to lead and excel is natural and right. Because men are gregarious, they need leadership for their social groups, and social progress depends largely on securing adequate leaders. Those who have the natural gifts for leadership—and also those who merely think they have—usually have a keen desire for its satisfactions. College life is a miniature world of criss-cross ambitions and of contrivances for trying out leaders.

Jesus did not demand self-effacement and the suppression of ability. He welcomed evidences of noble self-assertion. His own Messianic call was a summons to the highest leadership. His temptations were the settlement of leadership problems. His final lament over the city of Jerusalem was a burst of sorrow because he had failed to win his people to follow him.

Now, in moving about among men to win them for the Kingdom, Jesus encountered the leaders who were on deck before he came—the wealthy men who controlled the economic outfit; the official groups who held what political power was left to the Jews; and the lawyers, theologians, priests, and zealots who dominated the religious life of a very religious people. These classes overlapped; together they constituted the oligarchy of his nation. Both sides soon realized that there were fundamental antagonisms between them. The conflict grew acute, until it headed up in the great duel of the last days at Jerusalem. His experiences in this conflict with hostile leadership are recorded in the passages which we have studied and others like them.

II

In the fundamental reply to James and John he formulated his observations in a great political generalization: "Ye know that the rulers of the nations lord it over them and their great men hold down the rest by force." In its earlier and cruder forms, the State is a contrivance of a victorious group to hold down the conquered, and exploit them. If anyone has not yet read political history as an account of systematic exploitation of nation by nation and class by class, he has some education still coming to him.

Even where political leadership has not been plainly predatory but rested on real service, humanity has often had a heavy price to pay for it. Successful military leaders were able to perpetuate a royal dynasty and perhaps fasten a race of hereditary incapables on a nation, to be maintained in royal splendor. The feudal nobility performed useful work in the earlier, turbulent times, but it continued to take rent and tribute for centuries after its useful functions had lapsed. Modern business men who have organized public service corporations have often served the nation well, but they now own the highways and fundamental outfit of the nation, and if their descendants or assignees collect tribute, perhaps on inflated capitalization, for generations to come, it looks like rather costly service. The obligations of power have a curious way of getting lost in the shuffle of time, but titles, rank, legal privileges, rent, and interest are carefully groomed. If one man loses them, some other man nurses them, and the people always pay.

The Kingdom of God sets a fraternal and righteous social order against the predatory and unrighteous order which humanity has inherited from the past. The new order must have a new dynasty of leaders, for every social order has its own kind of aristocracy. Jesus does not propose to abolish leadership, but he proposes a new basis for greatness which is sharply opposed to the old: "Whoever has ambition to be a great man among you, let him be your servant; and whoever is ambitious to rank first among you, let him be your bondservant. Just as the Son of Man did not come to have others serve him, but to render service and to give his life as a ransom for many." Ability and ambition are still to lead, but they are to be yoked to the service of all. Not he who kills and subjugates, but he who makes life safe and happy, shall have the statue set up in his honor. Not the great warrior and killer, but the great healer and the man who multiplies the blades of grass and the ears of wheat and the size of potatoes shall be the great names treasured. The higher the honor craved, the more strenuous must be the service; if a man wants first prize, he must get down to voluntary slavery. The old way to leadership was to knock others down and climb up on them; the new way is to get underneath and boost.

III

Jesus put himself under this law of leadership. We see from his words that the cross was the outcome of a consistent principle adopted by him. The rules he laid down for his apostolate were meant to bar out selfish acquisition: "Freely ye received, freely give. Get you no gold, nor silver, nor brass in your purses; no wallet for your journey, neither two coats, nor shoes, nor staff; for the laborer is worthy of his food." It is a significant fact that again and again religious leaders who really cared for the condition of the people, have tried to create a genuine leadership for them along the same lines; Francis of Assisi gathered his "little brothers"; Peter Waldus his Bible teachers; Wycliffe his "poor preachers"; John Wesley his local preachers and itinerants; William Booth his ensigns and captains with the big bass drum; and the entire foreign mission propaganda calls for leaders who will go to the people and offers them nothing but enough to live in health. Today practically the entire Christian ministry, one of the most important bodies of men, has come under the law of leadership for service. It was once, at least in its upper-class sections, rich with unearned incomes, pervaded by graft, and domineering in spirit; it is now a clean and plain-living profession; whatever its short-comings, graft and extortion are not of them.

The question is now, whether other professions will go through the same historical process of cleansing. The religious spirit has pioneering qualities; under its impulse men blaze the trail which broad social movements or historical developments follow later. Greedy leadership first seemed intolerable in the Church; after a time it may become intolerable in politics and business. The trend of civilization is toward intelligent service on plain pay. Educators, judges, scientists, doctors are on that basis now. It has become dishonorable for them to use their positions for a holdup. The great discoverers in the line of sero-therapy might have taken toll in golden streams, but they did not. It would have been contrary to the ethics of their profession. That means that their profession is on a Christian basis. Where graft is taken out of politics, officials become devoted public servants. The reproach has been made against a man of great ability that at the end of his life his name is not connected with any great cause or measure for the welfare of the people. Whether the judgment was just or not, that point of view is the one to take.

Can business be brought under the law of service? Or is commerce constitutionally incapable of it? There are many indications that a conscious spiritual change is coming over those men in business who have enough intellect and character to look beyond immediate needs. The type of business leadership which took millions out of filthy factory towns, wore out women and took the youth out of children, cleared twelve per cent from slum tenements, kept men and women from marriage by underpayment, and kept the cradle empty by high prices and fear of the future—this type of leadership is antiquated. It belongs to a pre-Christian and pagan age. It is only a question whether business leaders will voluntarily turn their back on such misuse of power or have a change forced on them. Those who mark time on the old methods will become moral derelicts, and their wealth will not forever screen their moral obtuseness.

The nation needs leaders who will persuade conservative farmers to use scientific methods; who will teach our wasteful people the value of self-restraint, and the beauty of co-operative buying and selling; who will teach our communities that it is a sin to rob our own children by leaving soil, water, and forests poorer than we found them; who will give the people good housing without taking the unearned increment; who will organize the dangerous industries for safety; who will place the relations of leaders and workers in industry on a basis of justice and goodwill so that industrial peace can be attained. Is such an object satisfying to a young man of business capacity, or does he want to build a million dollar house and populate it with one child? It is confessed that civilization has been succeeding on the technical side and failing on the ethical. The more the machinery of life is concentrated in the hands of a limited group of business leaders, the more important does the social enlightenment and moral objective of these leaders become to society. To which of the two types do we belong?

IV

Will a life of service satisfy the capable and call out their best powers for the service of humanity? Men will play the game according to the rules of the game. If humanity changes the rules, its strong men will still let out their energies, because they can not help it, and they will like themselves all the better for being on the side of their fellow-men. There is no pleasure in being isolated, eyed with resentment, and conscious of hardness. If ten per cent net means long hours, low wages, and repression, and if six per cent would mean good will and contentment, it might pay the leaders of industry to take less in dividends and take it out in the higher satisfactions.

For men of great ability this is the chance for enduring

fame. Who will remember the men that did nothing but amass wealth? Who of our presidents are remembered and loved? Those who suffered with and for the people.

The leadership of service validates its rightness by its intellectual results. Predatory and parasitic classes become intellectually sterile and ignorant of real life. A man who wants to serve men, must get close to them. If we carry a load uphill, we have to choose our footing, and will perforce become intimately acquainted with the law of gravitation. Nothing develops the intellect like heading a just cause and fighting for it.

Here, then, we have another social principle of Jesus. The ambition of the strong must be yoked to the service of society. Power and honor must be earned by distinguished and costly service. Progress along this direction marks the progress of the Kingdom of God. Extortionate and domineering leadership must be superseded where the Kingdom of God moves forward.

V

Does the life of our colleges and universities square with this principle? College men and women crave honor from their fellows, or their fraternities crave it for them vicariously. How do the "big men" in college win it? Do they win it by raising the standards of intellectual work for all? By making fun clean and honorable through the power of a clean public opinion? By creating a college spirit which will put manhood into every generation of Freshmen that plunges into it? Or do they win honor by organizing parties, by intoxicating themselves and others with frothy "social" successes, by acting for the gallery to see and applaud, and by wasting the dynamics of youth on shooting rockets that look like stars and come down like sticks? Such men are essentially selfish; even their service is self-seeking and deserves no honor from others. The more talented and attractive they are, the more damage do they do. They perpetuate their kind. If fraternities or honorary societies honor and reward that sort of leadership, they force individuals into futility, and reenforce the natural temptation to shallow work and display by the powerful pressure of socialized public opinion.

What has just been said applies to the inner life of the college group during its brief command over young men and women. But meanwhile the outside life is waiting for them. Society creates and finances the colleges and universities from the social fund created by those who work. A college man who toys with his work and fights those who want to make him work, ought to be demoted and his chance given to some workingman who has intellectual hunger and would use it. But even of the able and efficient college men society has a right to inquire whether it is training enemies and exploiters or friends and leaders. This question will be asked more and more insistently by democracy as it becomes intelligent. Christianity anticipates this inquiry by its appeal to the individual conscience. Every college man and woman should choose the principle on which he proposes to exercise leadership in case he wins it. Are we willing to gain wealth by impoverishing others? Are we willing to get pleasure by degrading others? Are we willing to gain power and freedom for ourselves by making others powerless and unfree? Jesus distinguishes three kinds of men who are interested in the sheep—the robber, the hireling, and the shepherd. You can tell the presence of the robber by the death of the sheep; the hireling by his cowardice; the true leader by his valor and love.

A special word should be said to college women. In her book on "Woman and Labor," Olive Schreiner has pointed out that as families rise to wealth, the women slip into parasitism more readily than the men. They cease to do productive work, accept the luxuries of life as their right, and fall in with upper-class pretensions. The means of leadership—time, wealth, social resources—are at their command. How will they use them? The number of women with unearned incomes is increasing rapidly in America. Now, if much is given them, much will be required. Can they produce enough social values to justify what they consume? The least we can do is to give as much as we get. Anything less is immoral.

What kind of influence do college girls exert on able young men who turn toward them in love? Nothing will shrivel the idealistic conceptions of life in a young man as thoroughly as love for a selfish woman. The world is full of eyeless Samsons, grinding the money-mills, and whipped to a quicker pace by smiling grafters—who would not recognize this description of them if they saw it.

SUGGESTIONS FOR THOUGHT AND DISCUSSION

I. *The Need of Leadership*

1. Does the need of leadership diminish with the spread of democracy? With the growth of education?
2. Do we need leadership more or less in America today than fifty years ago?

II. *Jesus on the Problems of Leadership*

1. Give proof that Jesus consciously confronted the problem of social leadership.
2. What elements did he condemn in the old leadership of his nation?
3. What principle of leadership did he lay down for the new social order?
4. What body of leaders did he create, and what standards of special honor did he impose on them?
5. What do we think of the historic effectiveness of the leadership he created? What is the true interpretation of Judas Iscariot?
6. What evidences are there in Jesus' career that he was true to his ideals of leadership?

III. *The Problem of Leadership in History*

1. How have the great leaders in the field of religion attacked the problem of leadership in the Church? What does the Protestant Reformation signify from this point of view?

2. How have the landed aristocrats of the past met the Christian test of leadership?

3. Give examples from history and from modern life of men who exercised power in the way Christ condemned. Give examples of others who exercised it according to Christ's law.

IV. *The Problem of Leadership in Modern Life*

1. In what professions is ambition now securely tied up with service, so that a man must serve well in order to rise?

2. In what positions can a man still gain power and wealth by exploiting society?

3. Is the consciousness that they are public servants spreading among business men? If so, to what is this due?

4. Is society paying too big a price for the leadership of the industrial aristocracy today?

5. When the interests of the stockholders are set over against the health of women and children, and the safety of employes, which consideration determines the wages paid?

6. How have the social leaders of the past mortgaged the economic resources of nations to their own families? To what extent is this true of our country?

7. How can society protect itself against exploitation under present conditions?

V. *For Special Discussion*

1. A corporation has averaged 24 per cent to its stockholders. It pays twelve dollars a week to its ordinary

workmen. Would you call this predatory leadership? Where do you draw the line?

2. Does the salary of teachers in our country indicate that we honor according to service rendered?

3. How does the increasing size of business undertakings and their importance for public welfare emphasize the ethical importance of right leadership?

CHAPTER VIII
PRIVATE PROPERTY AND THE COMMON GOOD

Private Property Must Serve Social Welfare

A glance across history or a simple acquaintance with human life in any community will show us that private property is at the same time a necessary expression of personality and stimulator of character, and, on the other hand, a chief outlet and fortification of selfishness. Every reformatory effort must aim to conserve and spread the blessings of property, and every step toward a better social order will be pugnaciously blocked by its selfish beneficiaries.

What were Jesus' convictions about private property?

DAILY READINGS

FIRST DAY: *The Rival Interest*

And he spake to them many things in parables, saying, Behold, the sower went forth to sow; and as he sowed, some seeds fell by the way side, and the birds came and devoured them: and others fell upon the rocky places, where they had not much earth: and straightway they sprang up, because they had no deepness of earth: and when the sun was risen, they were scorched; and because they had no root, they withered away. And others fell upon the thorns; and the thorns grew up and choked them: and others fell upon the good ground, and yielded fruit, some a hundredfold, some sixty, some thirty. . . . When any one heareth the word of the kingdom, and understandeth it not, then cometh the

> evil one, and snatcheth away that which hath been sown in his heart. This is he that was sown by the way side. And he that was sown upon the rocky places, this is he that heareth the word, and straightway with joy receiveth it; yet hath he not root in himself, but endureth for a while; and when tribulation or persecution ariseth because of the word, straightway he stumbleth. And he that was sown among the thorns, this is he that heareth the word; and the care of the world, and the deceitfulness of riches, choke the word, and he becometh unfruitful. And he that was sown upon the good ground, this is he that heareth the word, and understandeth it; who verily beareth fruit, and bringeth forth, some a hundredfold, some sixty, some thirty.—Matt. 13: 3-8; 19-23.

This parable was intended to explain to the disciples why the Kingdom was not coming with a rush, as they expected. The story embodies the practical experiences of Jesus in his propaganda. He saw his work as a duplication of the sower's work on a higher level. The success of both depends on the receptiveness of the soil. The sower encounters hard trodden ground, rocky patches, and spots where hardy thorns or thistles drain the soil and where his work produces only empty ears and futile beginnings. So Jesus met the stolid conservative and also the emotional type. But the climax of his difficulties was a mind preoccupied by property worries, or lured by the illusions of wealth. He early found, then, that devotion to property is likely to be a rival to the higher interests and the common good.

How do modern social groups line up when measured by spiritual receptiveness?

SECOND DAY: *The Accumulator*

> And one out of the multitude said unto him, Teacher, bid my brother divide the inheritance with me. But he said unto him, Man, who made me a

judge or a divider over you? And he said unto them, Take heed, and keep yourselves from all covetousness: for a man's life consisteth not in the abundance of the things which he possesseth. And he spake a parable unto them, saying, The ground of a certain rich man brought forth plentifully: and he reasoned within himself, saying, What shall I do, because I have not where to bestow my fruits? And he said, This will I do: I will pull down my barns, and build greater; and there will I bestow all my grain and my goods. And I will say to my soul, Soul, thou hast much goods laid up for many years; take thine ease, eat, drink, be merry. But God said unto him, Thou foolish one, this night is thy soul required of thee; and the things which thou hast prepared, whose shall they be? So is he that layeth up treasure for himself, and is not rich toward God.—Luke 12: 13-21.

Most men today would have no fault to find with this man. He was only doing what the modern world is unanimously trying to do. Having made a pile, he proposed to make a bigger pile. Meanwhile he slapped his soul on the back and smacked his lips in anticipation. To Jesus the fat farmer was a tragic comedy. In the first place, an unseen hand was waiting to snuff out his candle. To plan life as if it consisted in an abundance of material wealth is something of a miscalculation in a world where death is part of the scheme of things. In the second place, Jesus saw no higher purpose in the man's aim and outlook to redeem his acquisitiveness. The man was a sublimated chipmunk, gloating over bushels of pignuts. If wealth is saved to raise and educate children, or achieve some social good, it deserves moral respect or admiration. But if the acquisitive instinct is without social feeling or vision, and centered on self, it gets no respect, at least from Jesus.

Unlimited acquisition used to be considered immoral and dishonorable. How and when did public opinion change on this?

THIRD DAY: *Quit Grafting*

> And the multitudes asked him, saying, What then
> must we do? And he answered and said unto them,
> He that hath two coats, let him impart to him that
> hath none; and he that hath food, let him do like-
> wise. And there came also publicans to be baptized,
> and they said unto him, Teacher, what must we do?
> And he said unto them, Extort no more than that
> which is appointed you. And soldiers also asked him,
> saying, And we, what must we do? And he said
> unto them, Extort from no man by violence, neither
> accuse any one wrongfully; and be content with your
> wages.—Luke 3: 10-14.

The social teachings of John the Baptist were so close
to those of Jesus that we can safely draw on them in this
passage.

John told the people that a new era was coming and they
would have to get a new mind and manner of life as an outfit
for it. The people asked for specifications. John's sugges-
tions ran along two lines. He encouraged the plain working
people to be neighborly and friendly, and share with a man
who was hard up. With powerful individuals, like hired
soldiers and Roman tax-farmers, he insisted that they must
quit using their physical force and legal power as a cinch
to extort money. In other words, they must quit grafting.
In the Kingdom of God the "big, black book of graft" will
be closed, and men will no longer eat their protesting fellow-
men. The more we realize that some form of graft is at
the bottom of most easy incomes, the more good sense will
we see in this kind of evangelism.

Have we ever been a victim of extortion? How did it
feel? Did it sour the milk of human kindness in us?

FOURTH DAY: *God versus Mammon*

> Lay not up for yourselves treasures upon the earth,
> where moth and rust consume, and where thieves

break through and steal: but lay up for yourselves
treasures in heaven, where neither moth nor rust
doth consume, and where thieves do not break
through nor steal: for where thy treasure is there
will thy heart be also. The lamp of the body is the
eye: if therefore thine eye be single, thy whole body
shall be full of light. But if thine eye be evil, thy
whole body shall be full of darkness. If therefore
the light that is in thee be darkness, how great is the
darkness! No man can serve two masters: for either
he will hate the one, and love the other; or else he
will hold to one, and despise the other. Ye cannot
serve God and mammon.—Matt. 6: 19-24.

Acquisition may operate on different planes. A man may
accumulate material stuff, or he may acquire spiritual facul-
ties, memories, and relations. In a balanced life the two work
side by side in peace, and each may aid the other. But the
experience of all spiritual teachers shows that practically
the acquisition of property often becomes a passion which
absorbs the man and leaves little energy for the higher pur-
suits. Most men who have used up their life to acquire
wealth look back with homesickness to some idealistic aspiration of their youth as to a lost Edenland. Jesus felt the
antagonism of private wealth and the Kingdom of God so
keenly that he set God and Mammon over against each
other, and warned us that we must choose between them.
Placed in this connection, the saying about the darkening of
the inner light seems to refer to the influence of money-
getting on the higher vision of the soul. This entire passage
is fundamental and will explain other sayings which follow.

Do God and money come into flat collision in college life?

FIFTH DAY: *The Divisive Influence of Riches*

Now there was a certain rich man, and he was
clothed in purple and fine linen, faring sumptuously
every day: and a certain beggar named Lazarus was
laid at his gate, full of sores, and desiring to be fed

with the crumbs that fell from the rich man's table;
yea, even the dogs came and licked his sores. And
it came to pass, that the beggar died, and that he was
carried away by the angels into Abraham's bosom:
and the rich man also died, and was buried. And in
Hades he lifted up his eyes, being in torments, and
seeth Abraham afar off, and Lazarus in his bosom.
And he cried and said, Father Abraham, have mercy
on me, and send Lazarus, that he may dip the tip of
his finger in water, and cool my tongue; for I am
in anguish in this flame. But Abraham said, Son,
remember that thou in thy lifetime receivedst thy
good things, and Lazarus in like manner evil things:
but now here he is comforted, and thou art in anguish.
And besides all this, between us and you there is a
great gulf fixed, that they that would pass from
hence to you may not be able, and that none may
cross over from thence to us. And he said, I pray
thee therefore, father, that thou wouldest send him
to my father's house; for I have five brethren; that
he may testify unto them, lest they also come into
this place of torment. But Abraham saith, They have
Moses and the prophets; let them hear them. And
he said, Nay, father Abraham: but if one go to them
from the dead, they will repent. And he said unto
him, If they hear not Moses and the prophets, neither
will they be persuaded, if one rise from the dead.
—Luke 16: 19-31.

Why does Jesus send the rich man to hell as if it were a
matter of course? No crimes or vices are alleged. It must
be that a life given over to sumptuous living and indifferent
to the want and misery of a fellow-man at the doorstep
seemed to Jesus a deeply immoral and sinful life. Jesus
exerted all his energies to bring men close together in love.
But wealth divides. It creates semi-human relations between
social classes, so that a small dole seems to be a full discharge of obligations toward the poor, and manly independence and virtue may be resented as offensive. The sting
of this parable is in the reference to the five brothers who

were still living as Dives had lived, and whom he was vainly trying to reach by wireless. See verse 14 in explanation.

Is it fair to call the relations between the selfish rich and the dependent poor "semi-human relations"?

SIXTH DAY: *Get a Plank for the Deluge*

And he said also unto the disciples, There was a certain rich man, who had a steward; and the same was accused unto him that he was wasting his goods. And he called him, and said unto him, What is this that I hear of thee? render the account of thy stewardship; for thou canst be no longer steward. And the steward said within himself, What shall I do, seeing that my lord taketh away the stewardship from me? I have not strength to dig; to beg I am ashamed. I am resolved what to do, that, when I am put out of the stewardship, they may receive me into their houses. And calling to him each one of his lord's debtors, he said to the first, How much owest thou unto my lord? And he said, A hundred measures of oil. And he said unto him, Take thy bond, and sit down quickly and write fifty. Then said he to another, And how much owest thou? And he said, A hundred measures of wheat. He saith unto him, Take thy bond, and write fourscore. And his lord commended the unrighteous steward because he had done wisely: for the sons of this world are for their own generation wiser than the sons of the light. And I say unto you, Make to yourselves friends by means of the mammon of unrighteousness; that, when it shall fail, they may receive you into the eternal tabernacles.—Luke 16: 1-9.

This is one of the wittiest stories in the Bible and must be read with some sense of humor. The tenant farmers of a great estate paid their rent in shares of the produce. This elastic system offered the steward a chance to make something on the side. He was found out and discharged, but while he was closing up his accounts he still had a short spell of authority. Things looked dark. He did not care to blister his white hands with a hoe-handle, nor his social pride by begging. So he grafted one last graft, but on so large a scale that the tenants would be under lasting obligations to him. The scamp was a crook, but at least he was long-headed. Jesus wished the children of light were as clever in taking a long look ahead as the children of this world. In that case men would get ready for the new age, in which mammon loses its buying power, by making friends with it now, and their friends would take them in as guests after the great reversal.

How do you like the humorous independence of Jesus?

SEVENTH DAY: *Stranded on His Wealth*

And a certain ruler asked him, saying, Good Teacher, what shall I do to inherit eternal life? And Jesus said unto him, Why callest thou me good? none is good, save one, even God. Thou knowest the commandments, Do not commit adultery, Do not kill, Do not steal, Do not bear false witness, Honor thy father and mother. And he said, All these things have I observed from my youth up. And when Jesus heard it, he said unto him, One thing thou lackest yet: sell all that thou hast, and distribute unto the poor, and thou shalt have treasure in heaven: and come, follow me. But when he heard these things, he became exceeding sorrowful; for he was very rich. And Jesus seeing him said, How hardly shall they that have riches enter into the kingdom of God! For it is easier for a camel to enter in through a needle's eye, than for a rich man to enter into the kingdom of God.—Luke 18: 18-25.

A fine young man, of clean and conscientious life, but with unsatisfied aspirations in his soul. Jesus invites him to a more heroic type of excellence, cutting loose from his wealth and devoting himself to the apostolate of the King-dom of God. It was a great chance for a great life. He might have stood for God before kings and mobs, and ranked with Peter, John, and Paul as a household name. He did not rise to his chance. What held him? Jesus felt it was his wealth. A poor man would have had less to leave, and might have left it cheerfully. So Jesus sums up the psychological situation in the saddened exclamation that it is exceedingly hard for a rich man to enter the Kingdom where men live in justice, fraternity, and idealism.

Have you noticed that in recent years an increasing number of this man's grandsons are trying to cut loose and find the real life, eternal life? Can you name any?

STUDY FOR THE WEEK

Evidently the dangers connected with property were much in the mind of Jesus. He seems to have emphasized them more fully and frequently than the evils of licentiousness or drunkenness. The modern Church has reversed the relative emphasis. Why?

Of course we must not look for the methods or viewpoints of political economy in his teachings. His concern was for the spiritual vitality and soundness of the individual, and for the human relations existing among men. He was interested in property only in so far as it corrupted the higher nature or made fraternity difficult. But let no one underestimate the importance of these considerations. These things are the real end of life. All the rest is scaffolding. We should be farther along if the economic and social sciences had kept these fundamental questions more sternly in sight.

I

Plainly Jesus felt that the acquisitive instinct, like the sex instinct, easily breaks bounds and becomes ravenous; there is even less natural limit to it. It absorbs the energies of intellect and will. As with the rich fool, the horizon of life is filled with chances to make the pile grow bigger. Life seems to consist of money, and the problems of money.

People are valued according to that standard. Marriages are arranged for it. Politics is run for it. Wars are begun for it. Creative artistic and intellectual impulses are shouldered aside, fall asleep, or die of inanition. Property is intended to secure freedom of action and self-development; in fact, it often chains men and clips their wings. This is what Jesus calls "the deceitfulness of riches" and "the darkening of the inner eye."[1]

In addition to the blight of character, wealth exerts a de-socializing and divisive influence. It wedges apart groups that belong together. Dives and Lazarus may live in the front and rear of the same block, but with no sense of solidarity. Dives would have been deeply moved, perhaps, if one of his own class had punctured a tire in the Philistian desert and gone for two days without any food except crumbs. The separation of humanity into classes on the lines of wealth is so universal and so orthodox that few of us ever realize that it flouts all the principles of Christianity and humanity.

In the case of the young ruler Jesus encountered the fact that wealth bars men out of the world of their ideals. The question was not whether the young man could get to heaven, but whether he could have a share in the real life, in the kingdom of right relations. It is hard to acquire great wealth without doing injustice to others; it is hard to possess it and yet deal with others on the basis of equal humanity; it is hard to give it away even without doing mischief.

We have seen that Jesus believed profoundly in the value and dignity of human life; that he sought to create solidarity; that he was chiefly concerned for the saving of the lowly; and that he demanded an heroic life in the service of the Kingdom of God. But wealth, as he saw it, flouted the value of life, dissolved the spiritual solidarity of whole classes, and kept the lowly low; the wealthy had lost the capacity for an heroic life.

[1] See the chapter on "The Tragedy of Dives" in Rauschenbusch, "Christianizing the Social Order," p. 291.

This is radical teaching. What shall we say to it? Jesus is backed by the Old Testament prophets and the most spiritual teaching of the Hebrew people, which condemned injustice and extortionate money-making even more energetically than did Jesus. Medieval Christianity sincerely assented to the principle that private property is a danger to the soul and a neutralizer of love. Every monastic community tried to cut under sex dangers by celibacy, and property dangers by communism. This was an enormous misinterpretation of Christianity, but it shows that men took the teachings on the dangers of private property seriously. The modern Christian world does not. It has quietly set aside the ideas of Jesus on this subject, lives its life without much influence from them, and contents itself with emphasizing other aspects.

Has the teaching of Jesus on private property been superseded by a better understanding of the social value of property? Or has his teaching been suppressed and swamped by the universal covetousness of modern life? "Our moral pace-setters strike at bad personal habits, but act as if there was something sacred about money-getting; and, *seeing that the master iniquities of our time are connected with money-making,* they do not get into the fight at all. The child-drivers, monopoly-builders, and crooked financiers have no fear of men whose thought is run in the moulds of their grandfathers. Go to the tainted-money colleges, and you will learn that Drink, not Graft, is the nation's bane" (Edward A. Ross, "Sin and Society, an Analysis of Latter-day Iniquity," p. 97—the italics are his).

II

The machinery for making money which Jesus knew, was simple, crude, and puny compared with the complicated and pervasive system which the magnates of modern industry have built up. There was probably not a millionaire in all Palestine. What would he have said to our great cities?

We need a Christian ethics of property, more perhaps than anything else. The wrongs connected with wealth are the most vulnerable point of our civilization. Unless we can make that crooked place straight, all our charities and religion are involved in hypocrisy.

We have to harmonize the two facts, that wealth is good and necessary, and that wealth is a danger to its possessor and to society. On the one hand property is indispensable to personal freedom, to all higher individuality, and to self-realization; the right to property is a corollary of the right to life; without property men are at the mercy of nature and in bondage to those who have property. On the other hand property is used as a means of collecting tribute and private taxes, as a club with which to extort unearned gain from laborers and consumers, and as the fundamental tool of oppression.

Where do we draw the line? Is it true that property created by productive labor is a great moralizer, and that property acquired without productive labor is the great demoralizer? Is it correct that property for use is on the whole good, and property for power is a menace?

What is the relation between property and self-development? At what point does property become excessive? At what point does food become excessive and poisonous? At what point does fertilizer begin to kill a plant? Would any real social values be lost if incomes averaged $2,000 and none exceeded $10,000?

To what extent does a moral purpose take the dangers out of acquisition?

Is any life moral in which the natural capacities are not sincerely taxed to do productive work? If a man's wealth is destined to cut his descendants off from productive labor, is it a blessing? What is the moral difference between strenuous occupation and labor? How large a proportion of our time and energy can be devoted to play and leisure without softening our moral fiber?

At what points does private property come to be anti-social? If we could eliminate the monopoly elements and the capacity to levy tribute, would there be much danger in the remainder?

Does private property, in the enormous aggregations of today and in control of the essential outfit of society, still correspond to the essential theoretical conception of private property, or have public properties and public functions fallen under private control? "Much that we are accustomed to hear called legitimate insistence upon the rights of property, the Old Testament would seem to call the robbery of God and grinding the faces of the poor" (The Bishop of Oxford).

III

The religious spirit will always have to call the individual farther than the law can compel him to go. After all unjust and tainted portions have been eliminated from our property, religion lays its hands on the rest and says, "You are only a steward over this." In the parables of the talents, the pounds, and the unjust steward, Jesus argues on the assumption that our resources are a trust, and not absolute property. We manage and control them, but always under responsibility. We hold them from God, and his will has eminent domain. But the will of God is identical with the good of mankind. When we hold property in trust for God, we hold it for humanity, of which we are part. We misuse the trust if by it we deprive others of health, freedom, joy, hope, or efficiency, for instance, by overworking others and underworking our own children.

SUGGESTIONS FOR THOUGHT AND DISCUSSION

I. *The Love of Money*

1. Define graft. What is wrong in it? Where do we see it? Where are we myopic about it?

2. Why did Jesus have so much to say about money and so little about drink? Why does Paul call the love of money "the root of all evil"?

II. *Jesus' Fear of Riches*

1. On what ground does Jesus fear the influence of riches and of their accumulation?

2. Summarize Jesus' teachings regarding wealth.

3. In what respects is his attitude different from the ordinary viewpoint of the modern world?

4. Was Jesus opposed to the owning of farming tools or fishing smacks? Where would he draw the line between honest earnings and dangerous wealth?

5. Was his teaching on wealth ascetic? Was it socialistic?

6. To what extent should we recognize his insight on this question as authority for us?

III. *The Problem of Wealth in the Modern World*

1. Are the "master iniquities" of our age located in sex life, politics, or business?

2. Distinguish between "property for use" and "property for power."

3. What are the moral evils created by mass poverty? By aggregations of wealthy families?

4. Why has the modern world set aside Jesus' teachings about wealth? To what extent have we substituted a better understanding of the social value of property? How far should we be satisfied with our present adjustment of the property question?

5. What methods of money making are condemned by the common sentiment of the Church? Is there anything which ought to be included in this condemnation? If so, what?

IV. *The Christian Attitude Toward Property and Wealth Under Modern Conditions*

1. At what point does the amassing of private property become contrary to the principles of Jesus?

2. What legalized property rights are antagonistic to Jesus' principles?

3. How can society accumulate wealth without the injustice and social divisions which now accompany the amassing of private fortunes?

4. If a man has an invested income, has he the right to live a life of leisure? When is it right to be a non-producer?

5. How rich has a Christian a right to be? In a Christian society what is the minimum limit of income?

6. Would economic democracy eliminate or enforce the doctrine of stewardship?

7. How can we pluck the sting of sin out of private property?

V. *For Special Discussion*

1. Are millionaires a symptom of social disease or a triumph of civilization?

2. Should social science reckon with the influence of wealth on personal character?

3. What moral conviction is expressed in the condemnation of usurious interest and of rack-rent? Should excessive profit be included?

4. How could industry be financed if there were no wealthy investors with accumulations?

5. When is a college student a parasite?

6. If college communities had less money would they breed better men and women?

7. How have the successes of predatory finance affected the outlook and morality of college students?

CHAPTER IX

THE SOCIAL TEST OF RELIGION

Religion Must be Socially Efficient

The teaching of Jesus dealt with three recalcitrant forces, which easily escape from the control of social duty and become a clog to spiritual progress: ambition for power and leadership, and the love of property, have been considered. How about religion? Is it a help or a hindrance in the progress of humanity? Opinions are very much divided today. No student of society can neglect religion as a social force. What did Jesus think of it?

DAILY READINGS

FIRST DAY: *Worship is not Enough*

What unto me is the multitude of your sacrifices? saith Jehovah: I have had enough of the burnt-offerings of rams, and the fat of fed beasts; and I delight not in the blood of bullocks, or of lambs, or of he-goats. When ye come to appear before me, who hath required this at your hand, to trample my courts? Bring no more vain oblations; incense is an abomination unto me; new moon and sabbath, the calling of assemblies,—I cannot away with iniquity and the solemn meeting. Your new moons and your appointed feasts my soul hateth; they are a trouble unto me; I am weary of bearing them. And when ye spread forth your hands, I will hide mine eyes from you; yea, when ye make many prayers, I will not hear: your hands are full of blood. Wash you, make you clean; put away the evil of your doings from before mine eyes; cease to do evil;

learn to do well; seek justice, relieve the oppressed, judge the fatherless, plead for the widow.—Isa. 1: 11-17.

Wherewith shall I come before Jehovah, and bow myself before the high God? shall I come before him with burnt-offerings, with calves a year old? will Jehovah be pleased with thousands of rams, or with ten thousands of rivers of oil? shall I give my first-born for my transgression, the fruit of my body for the sin of my soul? He hath showed thee, O man, what is good; and what doth Jehovah require of thee, but to do justly, and to love kindness, and to walk humbly with thy God?—Micah 6: 6-8.

These two passages are classical expressions of a note which runs through all the prophetic teaching of the Old Testament. There was a fundamental antagonism between those who saw the service of God in the inherited ritual and sacrificial action, and those who felt that the essential service of God is righteousness of life. The prophets wanted a religion that would change social conduct, and repudiated religious doings that had no ethical value. They held that worship alone is not enough. God wants life and conduct.

Suggest parallels from the history of the Christian or the non-Christian religions.

1- 26-20

SECOND DAY: *The Test of Social Value*

And it came to pass, that he was going on the sabbath day through the grainfields; and his disciples began, as they went, to pluck the ears. And the Pharisees said unto him, Behold, why do they on the sabbath day that which is not lawful? And he said unto them, Did ye never read what David did, when he had need, and was hungry, he, and they that were with him? How he entered into the house of God when Abiathar was high priest, and ate the showbread, which it is not lawful to eat save for the priests, and gave also to them that were with him? And he said unto them, The sabbath was made for man, and not man for the sabbath: so that the Son of man is lord even of the sabbath.

And he entered again into the synagogue; and there was a man there who had his hand withered. And they watched him, whether he would heal him on the sabbath day; that they might accuse him. And he saith unto the man that had his hand withered, Stand forth. And he saith unto them, Is it lawful on the sabbath day to do good, or to do harm? to save a life, or to kill? But they held their peace. And when he had looked round about on them with anger, being grieved at the hardening of their heart, he saith unto the man, Stretch forth thy hand. And he stretched it forth; and his hand was restored.—Mark 2 : 23-3 : 5.

The Mosaic law intended the Sabbath to be a haven of rest for all who were driven, the slave, the immigrant, even the cattle. It was a precious institution of social protection. But the strict religionists of Jesus' time had made a yoke of tyranny of it, so that hungry men could not rub the kernels from ears of grain without being charged with threshing, and Jesus could not heal a poor paralytic without getting black looks. A fine institution of social welfare and relief had been turned into an anti-social regulation. Jesus fell back on the fundamental maxim of the prophets, "I desire kindness and not sacrifice," and laid down the principle that "the Sabbath was made for man, and not man for the Sabbath." The religious institution of the Sabbath must have social value; this is the essential test even in religion.

Is the Sabbath more useful to society now than in Puritan times?

From which do we suffer more today, from excessive strictness or excessive looseness in Sabbath observance? *America*

How is the social value of the rest-day frustrated for the *mag* working class?

Sabbath for Man

Run services all day long.

2-19 2 o

THIRD DAY: *Natural Duty above Artificial*

And the Pharisees and the scribes ask him, Why walk not thy disciples according to the tradition of the elders, but eat their bread with defiled hands? And he said unto them, Well did Isaiah prophesy of you hypocrites, as it is written,

This people honoreth me with their lips,
But their heart is far from me.
But in vain do they worship me,
Teaching as their doctrines the precepts of men.

Ye leave the commandment of God, and hold fast the tradition of men. And he said unto them, Full well do ye reject the commandment of God, that ye may keep your tradition. For Moses said, Honor thy father and thy mother; and, He that speaketh evil of father or mother, let him die the death: but ye say, If a man shall say to his father or his mother, That wherewith thou mightest have been profited by me is Corban, that is to say, Given to God; ye no longer suffer him to do aught for his father or his mother; making void the word of God by your tradition, which ye have delivered: and many such like things ye do.—Mark 7: 5-13.

Contemporary Jewish religion was full of taboos, defilements, and purifications. Read Mark 7: 1-23. Jesus was so indifferent about the religious ablutions that he was brought to book for it by the pious. He replied that these regulations were not part of the divine law, but later accretions, the product of theological casuistry, and that they tended to obscure the real divine duties. He cited a flagrant case. By eternal and divine law a man owes love and support to his parents. But the scribes held that if a man vowed to give money to the temple, this obligation, being toward God, superseded the obligation to his parents, which was merely human. To Jesus this seemed a perversion of religion. Ecclesiastical claims were made to stifle fundamental social duty. To Jesus the latter had incomparably higher value. Religion had become a social danger through such teaching.

Give proof from modern history that religious institutions may become injurious to social morality and welfare.

FOURTH DAY: *Religion Which Obscured Duty*

> Woe unto you, scribes and Pharisees, hypocrites! for ye tithe mint and anise and cummin, and have left undone the weightier matters of the law, justice, and mercy, and faith: but these ye ought to have done, and not to have left the other undone. Ye blind guides, that strain out the gnat, and swallow the camel!
>
> Woe unto you, scribes and Pharisees, hypocrites! for ye cleanse the outside of the cup and of the platter, but within they are full from extortion and excess. Thou blind Pharisee, cleanse first the inside of the cup and of the platter, that the outside thereof may become clean also.—Matt. 23: 23-26.
>
> Woe unto you, scribes and Pharisees, hypocrites! for ye compass sea and land to make one proselyte; and when he is become so, ye make him twofold more a son of hell than yourselves.—Matt. 23: 15.

The great invective of Jesus against the scribes and Pharisees (Matthew 23) deals wholly with the perversions of religion. In these verses he emphasizes the fact that the solemn importance attached to external minutiæ turned the attention of men from the really fundamental spiritual duties, such as justice, mercy, and good faith. As the blood was supposed to be the sacred element of life, it had to be drained off in butchering, and a drowned animal could not be eaten. Jesus wittily describes the Pharisee filtering out drowned gnats from the drinking water, but bolting some camel of a sin without blinking. The outside of the cup was kept scrupulously scoured, but the inside was filled with the products of rapacity and the material for luxurious excess. When religion had become of such a sort, even missionary activity became an actual damage, for the converts were turned into fanatical sticklers on trifles. In all this we can see him striking out for a kind of religion that would result in righteous conduct and have social value.

✓ *Have we had any experience of religion which obscured duty to us? Have we had any experience of religion which revealed duty to us?*

FIFTH DAY: *Religious Wonders and Social Realities*

And the Pharisees and Sadducees came, and trying him asked him to show them a sign from heaven. But he answered and said unto them, When it is evening, ye say, It will be fair weather: for the heaven is red. And in the morning, It will be foul weather to-day: for the heaven is red and lowering. Ye know how to discern the face of the heaven; but ye cannot discern the signs of the times. An evil and adulterous generation seeketh after a sign; and there shall no sign be given unto it, but the sign of Jonah. And he left them, and departed.—Matt. 16: 1-4.

This demand for a miracle pursued Jesus all through his teaching activity. He settled with it on principle in his desert temptation; he would not leap from the pinnacles of the temple, or do anything to turn his work into a holy circus. But the demand followed him to his death: "If thou art the Son of God, come down from the cross." A good, stunning miracle seemed a short cut to faith, the most convincing way of furnishing proof of his divine mission. Also, it would be mighty interesting. But he never catered to the demand. His power was only for the relief of suffering. He tried to keep his acts of healing private. In this passage he advised his opponents to use their intellect in more useful directions than stargazing for signs from heaven. They were weather-wise. Let them read the signs of the times. Storms were brewing on the horizon. Forty years later Titus destroyed Jerusalem and broke the back of the Jewish nation. The prophetic mind of Jesus saw it coming (Luke 19: 41-44).

If they had accepted his teaching of peace instead of getting intoxicated by the visions of revolutionary apocalypticism, the doom might have been averted. He was trying to bring their feet to the ground, turn their mind to realities. and make their religion socially efficient.

Would the sight of a miracle have effected a moral change in a Pharisee?

✓ How would religion be affected, if miraculous demonstrations could be furnished at will?

SIXTH DAY: *When Religion Separates Men*

> And as Jesus passed by from thence, he saw a man, called Matthew, sitting at the place of toll: and he saith unto him, Follow me. And he arose, and followed him.
>
> And it came to pass, as he sat at meat in the house, behold, many publicans and sinners came and sat down with Jesus and his disciples. And when the Pharisees saw it, they said unto his disciples, Why eateth your Teacher with the publicans and sinners? But when he heard it, he said, They that are whole have no need of a physician, but they that are sick. But go ye and learn what this meaneth, I desire mercy, and not sacrifice: for I came not to call the righteous, but sinners.—Matt. 9: 9-13.

The Jewish community, religious at the core, had a fringe of people who had failed to live up to the requirements of the Law. They came under the condemnation of the respectable people and of their own conscience, and drifted into the despised and vicious occupations. These were the "publicans and sinners," the "publicans and harlots," to whom the Gospels refer. A socially efficient religion would have prompted the good people to establish loving and saving contact with these people. Actually religion so accentuated the social divergence that the Pharisees were shocked when Jesus mingled in a friendly way with this class and even added one of them to his traveling companions. The parables of the lost coin, lost sheep, and prodigal son were spoken in reply to the slur, "This man receiveth sinners, and eateth with them" (Luke 15). The elder brother of the prodigal pictures this loveless and censorious religion.

Jesus crossed the line of demarcation and established social contact and friendliness, through which salvation could come to these religious derelicts. He quoted again the old saying of the prophets, "I desire mercy, and not sacrifice." God was not as much concerned about correct religious performances as the Pharisees thought, and a great deal more concerned about mercy for the fallen, and the simple human qualities which bring the strong and the weak together.

What experiences have we had of refusal to associate? Was the cleavage along lines of race, wealth, education, morals, or religion?

✓ *Has religion with us been an impulse toward men, or away from men?*

SEVENTH DAY: *Be Useful or Die*

> And he spake this parable; A certain man had a fig tree planted in his vineyard; and he came seeking fruit thereon, and found none. And he said unto the vinedresser, Behold, these three years I come seeking fruit on this fig tree, and find none: cut it down; why doth it also cumber the ground? And he answering saith unto him, Lord, let it alone this year also, till I shall dig about it, and dung it: and if it bear fruit thenceforth, well; but if not, thou shalt cut it down.—Luke 13: 6-9.

Jesus evidently had some interest in scientific agriculture. Both the owner and the vine-dresser in this parable were out for agricultural efficiency. The owner hated to see soil and space wasted; the vine-dresser was reluctant to sacrifice a tree, and proposed better tillage and more fertilizer. Taking this parable in connection with what precedes, we see that

Jesus was concerned about the future of his nation and its religion. Both would have to validate their right to exist; God could not have them cumber the ground. They must make good. This is the stern urge of the God whom we know in history and evolution, with the voice of Christ pleading for patience. But it is agreed between them that ultimately the law of fitness must rule. Religion can not bank on claims of antiquity alone. Every generation must find it newly efficient to create the social virtues then needed. Remember that this was spoken by a Jewish patriot and the supreme exponent of the Hebrew religion.

Give historical instances of the permanent downfall or decline of nations. Trace the connection between their fate and their religion.

STUDY FOR THE WEEK

Jesus Christ was the founder of the highest religion; he was himself the purest religious spirit known to us. Why, then, was he in opposition to religion? The clash between him and the representatives of organized religion was not occasional or superficial. It ran through his whole activity, was one of the dominant notes in his teaching, culminated in the great spiritual duel between him and the Jewish hierarchy in the last days at Jerusalem, and led directly to his crucifixion.

I

The opposition of Jesus was not, of course, against religion itself, but against religion as he found it. It was not directed against any departure from the legitimate order of the priesthood; nor against an improper ritual or wrong doctrine of sacrifices. In fact, it did not turn on any of the issues which were of such importance to the Church in later times. He criticized the most earnest religious men of his day because their religion harmed men instead of helping them. It was unsocial, or anti-social.

The Old Testament prophets also were in opposition to the priestly system of their time because it used up the religious interest of the people in ceremonial performances without ethical outcome. It diverted spiritual energy, by substituting lower religious requirements for the one fundamental thing which God required—righteousness in social and political life. They insisted over and over that Jehovah wants righteousness and wants nothing else. Their aim was to make religion and ethics one and inseparable. They struck for the social efficiency of religion.

At the time of Jesus the Jewish sacrifices had lost much of their religious importance. During the Exile they had lapsed. They were professional performances of one class. The numerous Jews scattered in other countries perhaps saw the temple once in a lifetime. Modern feeling in the first century was against bloody sacrifices. The recorded sayings of Jesus hardly mention them. On the other hand the daily life of the people was pervaded by little prescribed religious actions. The Sabbath with its ritual was punctiliously observed.[1] There were frequent days of fasting, religious ablutions and baths, long prayers to be recited several times daily, with prayer straps around the arm and forehead, and a tasseled cloth over the head. The exact performance of these things seemed an essential part of religion to the most earnest men.

We have seen how Jesus collided with these religious requirements and on what grounds. If men were deeply concerned about the taboo food that went into their bodies, they would not be concerned about the evil thoughts that arose in their souls. If they were taught to focus on petty duties, such as tithing, the great ethical principles and obligations moved to the outer field of vision and became blurred. The Sabbath, which had originated in merciful purpose toward the poor, had been turned into another burden. Religion, which ought to bring good men into saving contact

---

[1]Edersheim, "Life and Times of Jesus, the Messiah," Appendix XVII, give a detailed account of Sabbath regulations.

with the wayward by love, actually resulted in separating the two by a chasm of religious pride and censoriousness. A man-made and artificial religious performance, such as giving toward the support of the temple, crowded aside fundamental obligations written deep in the constitution of human society, such as filial reverence and family solidarity.

Other reformers have condemned religious practices be-cause they were departures from the holy Book or from primitive custom. Jesus, too, pointed out that some of these regulations were recent innovations. But the real standard by which he judged current religious questions was not ancient authority but the present good of men. The spiritual center on which he took his stand and from which he judged all things, was the Kingdom of God, the perfect social order. Even the ordinances of religion must justify themselves by making an effective contribution to the Kingdom of God. The Sabbath was made for man, and its observance must meet the test of service to man's welfare. It must function wholesomely. The candle must give light, or what is the use of it? The salt must be salty and preserve from decay, or it will be thrown out and trodden under foot. If the fig-tree bears no fruit, why is it allowed to use up space and crowd better plants off the soil? This, then, is Christ's test in matters of institutional religion. The Church and all its doings must serve the Kingdom of God.

II

The social efficiency of religion is a permanent social problem. What is the annual expense of maintaining the churches in the United States? How much capital is in-vested in the church buildings? (See U. S. Census Bulletin No. 103, of 1906.) How much care and interest and loving free-will labor does an average village community bestow on religion as compared with other objects? All men feel instinctively that religion exerts a profound and subtle in-fluence on the springs of conduct. Even those who denounce it, acknowledge at least its power for harm. Most of us know it as a power for good. But all history shows that this great spiritual force easily deteriorates. *Corruptio optimi pessima.*

Religion may develop an elaborate social apparatus of its own, wheels within wheels, and instead of being a dynamic of righteousness in the natural social relations of men, its energies may be consumed in driving its own machinery. Instead of being the power-house supplying the Kingdom of God among men with power and light, the Church may exist for its own sake. It then may become an expensive consumer of social wealth, a conservative clog, and a real hindrance of social progress.

Live religion gives proof of its value by the sense of freedom, peace, and elation which it creates. We feel we are right with the holy Power which is behind, and beneath, and above all things. It gives a satisfying interpretation of life and of our own place in it. It moves our aims higher up, draws our fellow-men closer, and invigorates our will.

But our growth sets a problem for our religion. The religion of childhood will not satisfy adolescent youth, and the religion of youth ought not to satisfy a mature man or woman. Our soul must build statelier mansions for itself. Religion must continue to answer all our present needs and inspire all our present functions. A person who has failed to adjust his religion to his growing powers and his intellectual horizon, has failed in one of the most important functions of growth, just as if his cranium failed to expand and to give room to his brain. Being microcephalous is a misfortune, and nothing to boast of.

Precisely the same problem arises when society passes through eras of growth. Religion must keep pace. The Church must pass the burning torch of religious experience from age to age, transmitting the faith of the fathers to the children, and not allowing any spiritual values to perish. But it must allow and aid religion to adjust itself. Its inspiring teaching must meet the new social problems so effectively that no evil can last long or grow beyond remedy. In every new age religion must stand the test of social efficiency. Is it passing that test in Western civilization?

Religion is a bond of social coherence. It creates loyalty. But it may teach loyalty to antiquated observances or a dwarfed system of truth. Have you ever seen believers rallying around a lost cause in religion? Yet these relics were once a live issue, and full of thrilling religious vitality.

Society changes. Will religion change with it? If society passes from agriculture and rural settlements to industry and urban conditions, can the customary practices of religion remain unchanged? Give some instances where prescientific conceptions of the universe, embodied in religion, have blocked the spread of scientific knowledge among the people. The caste distinctions of Hinduism were the product of a combination between religion and the social organization of the people; can they last when industrialism and democracy are pervading India? The clerical attitude of authority was natural when the Catholic clergy were the only educated class in the community; is it justified today? Protestantism won the allegiance of industrial communities when the young business class was struggling to emancipate itself from the feudal system. It developed an individualistic philosophy of ethics. Today society tends toward solidaristic organization. How will that affect religion and its scheme of duty? Thus religion, by its very virtues of loyalty and reverence, may fall behind and lose its full social efficiency. It must be geared to the big live issues of today if it is to manifest its full saving energies.

How does this problem of the efficiency of religion bear on the foreign missionary movement? How will backward or stationary civilizations be affected by the introduction of a modern and enthusiastic religion?

We may feel the defects of our church life at home, but there is no doubt that the young men and women who go out from our colleges under religious impulses, are felt as a virile and modernizing force when they settle to their work in Turkey or Persia. Christian educational institutions and medical missions have raised the intellectual and humane standards of young China. Buddhism in Japan has felt the challenge of competition and is readjusting its ethics and philosophy to connect with modern social ideals. The historical effects of our religious colonization will not mature for several generations, but they are bound to be very great. The nations and races are drawing together. They need a monotheistic religion as a spiritual basis for their sense of human unity. This is a big, modern, social task. It makes its claim on men and women who have youth, education, and spiritual power. Is the religious life of our colleges and universities efficient enough to meet the need?

Here are the enormous tasks of international relations, which the Great War has forced us to realize—the prevention of armed conflicts, the elimination of the irritant causes of war, the protection of the small nations which possess what the big nations covet, the freedom of the seas as the common highway of God, fair and free interchange in commerce without any effort to set up monopoly rights and the privilege of extortionate gain, the creation of an institutional basis for a great family of nations in days to come. These are some of the tasks which the men and women who are now young must take on their mind and conscience for life, and leave to their children to finish. What contributions, in your opinion, could the spirit of the Christian religion make to such a program, if it were realized intelligently and pressed home through the agencies of the Christian Church? In what ways has American religion shown its efficiency since the war broke out?

Christianity has been a great power in our country to cleanse and fraternalize the social life of simple communities. Can it meet the complex needs of modern industrialism in the same way? It can not truthfully be claimed that it has done so in any industrial country. Its immense spiritual forces might be the decisive element, but they have been effectively organized against a few only of the great modern evils. On the fundamental ethical questions of capitalism the Church has not yet made up its own mind—not to speak of enforcing the mind of Christ. Nor have the specialists in the universities and colleges supplied the leaders of the Church with clear information and guidance on these questions. We can not make much permanent progress toward a just social order as long as the masses of the working people in the industrial nations continue in economic poverty and political helplessness, and as long as a minority controls the land, the tools, and the political power. We shall linger on the borders of the Inferno until a new accession of moral insight and spiritual power comes to the nations. How will it come?

III

What could the churches in an average village community accomplish if they intelligently directed the power of religion to foster the sense of fraternal unity and to promote the institutions which make for unity? How could they draw the new, the strange, and the irregular families into the circle of neighborly feeling? In what way could they help to assimilate immigrants and to prevent the formation of several communities in the same section, overlapping, alien, and perhaps hostile? How would it affect the recreational situation if the churches took a constructive rather than a prohibitive attitude toward amusements, and if they promoted the sociability of the community rather than that of church groups?

With the rise of land prices and the control of transportation and markets, the rural population is moving toward a social crisis like that which transformed the urban population in the industrial revolution. Agriculture will become capitalistic, and the weaker families will drop to the position of tenants and agricultural laborers. Cooperation is their way of salvation. Its effectiveness has been amply demonstrated in older countries. It requires a strong sense of solidarity, loyalty, and good faith to succeed. It has made so little headway in America because our national character has not been developed in these directions. What could the churches do to save the weaker families from social submergence by backing cooperation and developing the moral qualities needed for it?

The strong religious life of our people might be more effective if the churches were less divided. Their economic and human resources are partly wasted by useless competition. Our denominational divisions are nearly all an historical heritage, imported from Europe, and coming down from a controversial age. Their issues all meant something vital and socially important in the midst of the social order of that day; but in many cases the real significance has quietly crumbled away, and they are not really the same issues that deeply engaged our forefathers. We are all "tithing mint, anise, and cummin," and forgetting the weighty matters, such as social justice and Christian fraternity. Everybody is ready to acknowledge this about every denomination except his own. We need a revaluation of our religious issues from the point of view of the Kingdom of God. That would bring us into harmony with the judgment of Jesus. Nothing else will.

IV

The social efficiency of religion—what call is there in that to the college men and women of this generation? Shall they cease to worship and pray, seek the salvation of society in ethics and sociology, and abandon religion to stagnation? Or shall they seek a new experience of religion in full sight of the modern world, and work by faith toward that reign of God in which his will shall be done?

Suggestions for Thought and Discussion

I. *When the Salt Loses its Savor*

   1. What is the individual to do when religion becomes a hindrance to religion?

2. What types of revolt against inherited religion have you met in college?

II. *Prophetic Religion Against Traditional Religion*

1. What did the prophets criticize in the religion of their day?

2. What was Jesus' test of religion?

3. Give instances in which he found religion to be a hindrance to the highest welfare. How did religion obscure duty?

4. What was the essential cause of the clash between Jesus and the religious leaders of his day?

III. *The Historic Reformation of Religion*

1. In studying history, what sins or failures of the Church have impressed you most?

2. What did the Protestant Reformation contribute to make religion efficient?

3. Has the Church been a rival or a feeder of the Kingdom of God?

4. Give historical examples of the failure of religion to meet the changed requirements of a new epoch.

5. What contributions has the Church made to social progress?

IV. *Religion Today*

1. What have Christian missions done to change the social conditions in non-Christian countries?

2. How do you rate the social service value of a first-class minister in a community? On what does his value depend?

3. Of what social value to a community is a costly and beautiful church building?

4. What investment in capital and annual expenditure does the maintenance of the churches in your community

entail? Does the social return to the community justify the investment?

5. Are the issues which divided the Protestant denominations in the sixteenth and seventeenth centuries still vital enough to justify the continuance of the divisions? Summarize the evils of the divisions and their counterbalancing good.

6. Is the ordinary criticism of the churches fair? Are ministers overpaid or underpaid? Do the churches graft? How do the churches compare in social efficiency with other similar social institutions?

V. *For Special Discussion*

1. Why did the reformation of the Church historically precede the reform of politics and industry?

2. Do the unsolved social problems of Christian nations prove the social inefficiency of religion? Could religion alone change the maladjustment of society?

3. Why has religion been more effective in the field of private life than of public life?

4. If you had full control of the churches in a given country or village community, on what aims would you concentrate their forces?

PART IV
CONQUEST BY CONFLICT

CHAPTER X

THE CONFLICT WITH EVIL

The Kingdom of God Will Have to Fight for Its Advance

The great objective is the Kingdom of God. In realizing the Reign of God on earth three recalcitrant forces have to be brought into obedience to God's law: the desire for power, the love of property, and unsocial religion. We have studied Christ's thought concerning these in the foregoing chapters. The advance of the Kingdom of God is not simply a process of social education, but a conflict with hostile forces which resist, neutralize, and defy whatever works toward the true social order. The strategy of the Kingdom of God, therefore, involves a study of the social problem of evil.

DAILY READINGS

FIRST DAY: *The Consciousness of Sin in the Lord's Prayer*

And forgive us our debts, as we also have forgiven our debtors. And bring us not into temptation, but deliver us from the evil one.—Matt. 6: 12, 13.

The Lord's Prayer expresses the very mind and spirit of the Master. It begins with the Kingdom of God; it ends with the problem of sin. As we stand before God, we realize that we have loaded up our life with debts we can never pay. We have wasted our time, and the powers of body and soul. We have left black marks of contagion on some whose path we have crossed. We have hurt even those who loved us by our ill-temper, thoughtlessness, and selfishness.

We can only ask God to forgive and give us another chance: "Forgive us our debts." Looking forward we see the possibility of fatal temptations. We know how fragile our power of resistance is. "Lead us not into temptation, but deliver us from evil." Thus the consciousness of sin is written across this greatest of all prayers.

Is a sense of unworthiness an indication of moral strength or of weakness?

Where do we draw the line between a normal and abnormal sense of sin?

SECOND DAY: *Evil Embodied in Character*

> Either make the tree good, and its fruit good; or make the tree corrupt, and its fruit corrupt: for the tree is known by its fruit. Ye offspring of vipers, how can ye, being evil, speak good things? for out of the abundance of the heart the mouth speaketh. The good man out of his good treasure bringeth forth good things: and the evil man out of his evil treasure bringeth forth evil things. And I say unto you, that every idle word that men shall speak, they shall give account thereof in the day of judgment. For by thy words thou shalt be justified, and by thy words thou shalt be condemned.—Matt. 12: 33-37.

Character is formed by action, but after it is formed, it determines action. What a man says and does, he becomes; and what he has become, he says and does. An honest and clean-minded man instinctively does what is kind and honorable. But when a man for years has gone for profit and selfish power, you can trust him as a general thing to do what is underhanded and mean. Since selfish ability elbows its way to controlling positions in business, politics, and society, the character reactions of such men are a force with which the Kingdom of God must reckon. They are the personal equipment of the kingdom of evil, and the more respectable, well-dressed, and clever they are, the worse it is.

What man or woman of our acquaintance would **we single** out as the clearest case of an evil character?

Why do we so judge him?

Third Day: *The Social Pressure of Evil*

> And he said unto his disciples, It is impossible but that occasions of stumbling should come; but woe unto him, through whom they come! It were well for him if a millstone were hanged about his neck, and he were thrown into the sea, rather than that he should cause one of these little ones to stumble.— Luke 17: 1, 2.

A sex story lodging in a young mind, an invitation to companionship and a drink, a sneer at religion which makes faith look silly—such things trip us up. They are stumbling-blocks, like wires stretched across a path in the dark. Just because we are social and easily influenced by friendship, admiration, or persuasion, one man's suggestion or example draws the other man on. Jesus knew that social solicitation and pressure toward sin was inevitable. It is the price we pay for our social nature. But, all the same, it is a terrible thing to contaminate a soul or steer a life toward its ruin. This saying about the millstone is one of the sternest words ever uttered.

> "Three men went out one summer night,
> No care they had or aim,
> And dined and drank. 'Ere we go home
> We'll have,' they said, 'a game.'
>
> Three girls began that summer night
> A life of endless shame,
> And went through drink, disease, and death,
> As swift as racing flame.
> Lawless and homeless, foul they died;
> Rich, loved, and praised the men;
> But when they all shall meet with God,
> And justice speaks—what then?"

Let us enumerate to our own minds cases where others drew us into wrong, and cases where we were a cause of evil for others. About which do we feel sorest now? Why?

FOURTH DAY: *Moral Laziness*

No man having drunk old wine desireth new; for he saith, The old is good.—Luke 5: 39.

This is a chance remark, but a keen observation. In wine-raising countries an expert tongue and nice discrimination between the fifty-seven varieties is one of the most coveted talents. A man who would prefer some recent stuff to the celebrated vintage of 18—, would commit intellectual *hari-kari*. It is said that in some of the celebrated vaults of France they breed spiders to cover the bottles with webs and dust to convey the delicious suggestion of antiquity. Jesus uses the preference for old vintage to characterize the conservative instinct in human nature. This is one of the stickiest impediments to progress, one of the most respectable forms of evil-mindedness. "The hereditary tiger is in us all, also the hereditary oyster and clam. Indifference is the largest factor, though not the ugliest form, in the production of evil" (President Hyde). Men are morally lazy; they have to be pushed into what is good for them, and the "pushee" is almost sure to resent the pushing. The idea that men ardently desire what is rational and noble is pernicious fiction. They want to be let alone. This is part of original sin.

Was the above written in haste, or will it stand?

FIFTH DAY: *Satanic Frustration of Good*

Another parable set he before them, saying, The kingdom of heaven is likened unto a man that sowed good seed in his field: but while men slept, his enemy came and sowed tares also among the wheat, and went away. But when the blade sprang up and brought forth fruit, then appeared the tares also. And the servants of the householder came and said unto him, Sir, didst thou not sow good seed in thy field? whence then hath it tares? And he said unto them, An enemy hath done this. And the servants say unto him, Wilt thou then that we go and gather them up? But he saith, Nay; lest haply while ye gather up the tares, ye root up the wheat with them. Let both grow together until the harvest: and in the time of the harvest I will say to the reapers, Gather up first the tares, and bind them in bundles to burn them; but gather the wheat into my barn.— Matt. 13: 24-30.

Here we encounter the devil. There is more in sin than our own frailty and stupidity, and the bad influence of other individuals. There is a permanent force of organized evil which vitiates every higher movement and sows tares among the grain over night. You work hard on some law to reform the ballot or the primary in order to protect the freedom and rights of the people, and after three years your device has become a favorite tool of the interests. You found a benevolent institution, and after you are dead it becomes a nest of graft. Even the Church of Jesus was for centuries so corrupt that all good men felt its reform in head and members to be the greatest desideratum in Christendom. Evil is more durable and versatile than youth and optimism imagine. The belief in a satanic power of evil expresses the conviction of the permanent power of evil. In early Christianity the belief in the devil was closely connected with the Christian opposition to the idolatrous and wicked social order of heathenism. In the Apocalypse the dragon who stands for Satan, and the beasts who stand for the despotic Roman Empire, are in close alliance.

What are the satanic social forces today?

The parable of the tares grew out of a personal experience. *Has our observation ever furnished anything similar?*

SIXTH DAY: *The Irrepressible Conflict*

Think not that I came to send peace on the earth: I came not to send peace, but a sword. For I came to set a man at variance against his father, and the daughter against her mother, and the daughter in law against her mother in law: and a man's foes shall be they of his own household. He that loveth father or mother more than me is not worthy of me; and he that loveth son or daughter more than me is not worthy of me. And he that doth not take his cross and follow after me, is not worthy of me. He that findeth his life shall lose it; and he that loseth his life for my sake shall find it.—Matt. 10: 34-39.

Into a world controlled by sin was launched the life of Christ. The more completely he embodied the divine character and will, the more certain and intense would be the conflict between him and the powers dominating the old order. He accepted this fight, not only for himself but for his followers. It would follow them up into the intimacies of their homes. Any faith that takes the Kingdom of God seriously, has its fight cut out for it. Unless we accept our share of it, we are playing with our discipleship. But when the fight is for the Kingdom of God, those who dodge, lose; and those who lose, win.

Which involves more conflict, a life set on the Kingdom of God on earth, or a faith set on the life to come?
Does the idea of a fighting faith attract us?
Would this serve as a "substitute for war"?

SEVENTH DAY: *Militant Gentleness*

But I say unto you, Love your enemies, and pray for them that persecute you; that ye may be sons of your Father who is in heaven: for he maketh his sun to rise on the evil and the good, and sendeth rain on the just and the unjust.—Matt. 5: 44, 45.

Render to no man evil for evil. Take thought for things honorable in the sight of all men. But

if thine enemy hunger, feed him; if he thirst, give
him to drink: for in so doing thou shalt heap coals
of fire upon his head. Be not overcome of evil, but
overcome evil with good.—Rom. 12: 17, 20, 21.

Jesus answered, My kingdom is not of this world:
if my kingdom were of this world, then would my
servants fight, that I should not be delivered to the
Jews: but now is my kingdom not from hence. Pilate
therefore said unto him, Art thou a king then? Jesus
answered, Thou sayest that I am a king. To this
end have I been born, and to this end am I come
into the world, that I should bear witness unto the
truth. Every one that is of the truth heareth my
voice.—John 18: 36, 37.

When we call out the militant spirit in religion, we summon a dangerous power. It has bred grimness and cruelty.
Crusaders and inquisitors did their work in the name of
Jesus, but not in his spirit. We must saturate ourselves with
the spirit of our Master if our fighting is to further his
Kingdom. Hate breeds hate; force challenges force. Only
love disarms; only forgiveness kills an enemy and leaves a
friend. Jesus blended gentleness and virility, forgiving love
and uncompromising boldness. He offered it as a mark of his
Kingdom that his followers used no force to defend him.
Wherever they have done so, the Kingdom of heaven has
dropped to the level of the brutal empires. His attack is by
the truth; whoever is won by that, is conquered for good.
Force merely changes the form of evil. When we "overcome
evil with good," we eliminate it.

What did Paul mean by saying that acts of kindness to
an enemy heap coals of fire on his head?

How about moral crusades that aim to put joint-keepers
and pimps in prison?

STUDY FOR THE WEEK

All great religious teachers have had a deep sense of the
power of evil in human life. Jesus apparently was not in-

terested in the philosophical question of the origin of evil, but accepted the fact of evil in a pragmatic way, and saw his own life as a conflict with sin and wrong.

Some facts, as we have seen, were clearly written in his consciousness: the frailty of our will; the consolidation of evil in men of bad character and the automatic output of lies and distortions coming from such; the power of social pressure by which the weak are made to trip and fall; and the pervasive satanic power of evil which purposely neutralizes the efforts leading toward the Reign of God.

The fact that Jesus realized evil in individuals and society, that he reckoned with it practically, and that he set himself against it with singleness of purpose, constitutes another of his social principles. Any view of life which blurs the fact of evil would have seemed to him an illusion. He would have foretold failure for any policy based on it. His great social problem was redemption from evil. Every step of approach toward the Kingdom of God must be won by conflict.

Modern science explains evil along totally different lines, but as to the main facts it agrees with the spiritual insight of Jesus. Psychology recognizes that the higher desires are usually sluggish and faint, while the animal appetites are strong and clamorous. Our will tires easily and readily yields to social pressure. In many individuals the raw material of character is terribly flawed by inheritance. So the young, with a maximum of desire and a minimum of self-restraint, slip into folly, and the aging backslide into shame. Human nature needs a strong reenforcement to rouse it from its inherited lethargy and put it on the toilsome upward track. It needs redemption, emancipation from slavery, a breaking of bonds.

I

Evangelism is the attack of redemptive energy in the sphere of personal life. It comes to a man shamed by the sense of guilt and baffled by moral failure, and rouses him to a consciousness of his high worth and eternal destiny. It transmits the faith of the Christian Church in a loving and gracious God who is willing to forgive and powerful to save. It teaches a man to pray, curing his soul by affirming over and over a triumphant faith, and throwing it open to mysterious spiritual powers which bring joy, peace, and strength beyond himself. It sets before him a code of moral duty to quicken and guide his conscience. It puts him inside of a group of like-minded people who exercise social restraint and urge him on.

When all this is wisely combined, it constitutes a spiritual reenforcement of incomparable energy. It acts like an emancipation. It gives a sense of freedom and newness. The untrained observer sees it mainly in those cases where the turn has come in some dramatic form and where the contrast between the old and new life is most demonstrable. But the saving force is at work even when it seeps in through home influences so quietly that the beneficiary of it does not realize what a great thing has been done for him.

The saving force has to attack the powers in possession. Only those who have helped in wresting men free from sin can tell what a stiff fight it often is. Here is an intellectual professional man who goes off for a secret spree about once in sixty days; a respectable woman who has come under the opium habit; a boy who is both a cigarette fiend and sexually weak; a man who domineers and cows his wife and family; a woman who has reduced her husband to slavery to supply her expensive tastes; a girl who shirks all work and throws the burden of her selfish life on a hard-worked mother; a college man whose parents are straining all their resources and using up their security for old age to keep him at college, and who gambles—complete the catalogue for yourself. To make these individuals over into true citizens of the Kingdom of God and loyal fellow-workers of their fellow-men means constructive conflict of a high order. It has been done.[1]

---

[1] See, for instance, Begbie, "Twice Born Men."

II

The problem of evil becomes far more complicated when evil is socialized. The simplest and most familiar form of that is the boys' gang. Here is a group of young humans who get their fun and adventure by pulling the whiskers of the law. They idealize vice and crime. Leadership in their group is won by proficiency in profanity, gambling, obscenity, and slugging. The gang assimilates its members; there is regimentation of evil. It acts as a channel of tradition; the boy of fifteen teaches the boy of twelve what he has learned from the boy of eighteen.

How is the problem of evil affected when the powers of human society, which usually restrain the individual from vice and rebellion, are used to urge him into it? Should the strategy of the Kingdom of God be adjusted to that situation? It is not enough to win individuals away from the gangs. Can the gang spirit itself be christianized and used to restrain and stimulate the young for good? Has this been done, and where, and how? Is Christian institutional work sufficient to cope with the problem? What readjustments in the recreational and educational outfit of our American communities are needed to give a wholesome outlet to the spirit of play and adventure, and to train the young for their life work? Would such an outfit do the work without personal leadership inspired by religion?

Christian evangelism in the past has not had an adequate understanding of the power of the group. In what connections has the Church shown a true valuation of the social factor in sin and redemption? At what points has its strategy been ineffective in dealing with socialized evil? What contributions can social science make to the efficiency of evangelism? Would a correct scientific analysis of the constructive and disintegrating forces in society be enough to do saving work?

III

The bad gangs of the young are usually held together by

a misdirected love of play and adventure. The dangerous combinations of adults are consolidated by "the cohesive power of plunder." That makes them a far more difficult proposition.

Any local attack on saloons and vice resorts furnishes a laboratory demonstration of socialized evil. The object of both kinds of institutions is to make big profit by catering to desires which induce men to spend freely. Music and sociability are used as a bait. The people who profit by this trade are held together by the fear of a common danger. Since the community uses political means of curbing or suppressing the vice business, the vice group goes into politics to prevent it. It seeks to control the police, the courts, the political machines by sharing part of its profits. Lawyers, officials, newspaper proprietors, and real estate men are linked up and summoned like a feudal levy in case of danger. Drugstores, doctors, chauffeurs, messenger boys, and all kinds of people are used to bring in trade and make it secure. The exploded fictions of alcoholism are kept circulating. Like a tape-worm in the intestines, these articulated and many-jointed parasitic organizations of vice make our communities sick, dirty, and decadent.

We have learned to read the sordid trail of the drink and vice traffic in American communities. There is another kind of organized evil, even more ancient, pervasive, and deadly, which few understand, though it has left a trail sufficiently terrible.

Wherever we look in the history of the older nations, we see an alignment of two fundamental classes. The one is born to toil, stunted by toil, and gets its class characteristics by toil. The other is characterized by the pleasures and arts of leisure, is physically and mentally developed by leisure, and proud and jealous of its leisure. This class is always class-conscious; its groups, however antagonistic, always stand together against the class of toil. Its combination of leisure and wealth is conditioned on the power of taking tribute from the labor of many. In order to do this

with safety, it must control political power, the military outfit, the power of making, interpreting and executing the laws,
and the forces forming public opinion.

Before the advent of industrialism and political democracy,
it secured its income by controlling the land and the government of nations; and the effects of its control can be read in
the condition of the rural population of Russia, Austria,
Eastern Germany, Italy, France before the Revolution, England, and especially Ireland. The development of industry
has changed the problem of economic and political control;
but the essentials remain, as we can see in the condition of
industrial communities and the history of labor legislation.

The fundamental sin of all dominant classes has been the
taking of unearned incomes. Political oppression has always
been a corollary of economic parasitism, a means to an end.
The combination of the two constitutes the largest and most
continuous form of organized evil in human history.

Jesus used the illustration of pegs maliciously driven into
the path to make men stumble and fall. It would require
some illustration drawn from modern machinery to express
the wholesale prostration of bodies and souls where covetousness has secured continuous power and has been able to
get in its full work. Anyone who has ever looked with
human understanding at the undersized and stupid peasants
of countries ruled by their landlord class, or at the sordid
homes and pleasures of miners or industrial workers where
some corporation feared neither God nor the law, ought to
get a comprehension of the power of evil that has rested like
an iron yoke on humanity.

We think most readily of the children of the poor as a
product of exploitation; underfed and overstimulated, cut
off from the clean pleasures of nature, often tainted with
vice before knowledge has come, and urged along by the
appetites and cruel selfishness of older persons, they are a
standing accusation against society itself.[2] Jesus would have

---

[2] See Jane Addams, "A New Conscience and an Ancient Evil."

felt that the children of the rich are an even worse product of exploitation than the poor. When "society" plays, it burns up the labor of thousands like fireworks. The only possible justification for the aggregations of wealth is that the rich are to act as the trustees and directors of the wealth of society; but their children—except in conspicuous and fine exceptions—are put out of contact with the people whom they must know if they are to serve them, so that it takes heroic effort on the part of noble exceptions to get in contact with the people once more, and to discover how they live. In all nations the atmosphere of the aristocratic groups drugs the sense of obligation, and possesses the mind with the notion that the life and labor of men are made to play tennis with. The existence of great permanent groups, feeding but not producing, dominating and directing the life of whole nations according to their own needs, may well seem a supreme proof of the power of evil in humanity.

IV

If evil is socialized, salvation must be socialized. The organization of the Christian Church is a recognition of the social factor in salvation. It is not enough to have God, and Christ, and the Bible. A group is needed, organized on Christian principles, and expressing the Christian spirit, which will assimilate the individual and gradually make him over into a citizen of the Kingdom of God. Salvation will rarely come to anyone without the mediation of some individual or group which already has salvation. It may be very small and simple. "Where two or three are gathered in my name, there am I in the midst of them." That saying recognizes that an additional force is given to religion by its embodiment in a group of believers. Professor Royce has recently reasserted in modern terms the old doctrine that "there is no salvation outside of the Church," calling the Church "the beloved community." Of course the question is how intensively Christian the Church can make its members. That will depend on the question how Christian the Church itself is, and there's the rub.

The Church is the permanent social factor in salvation. But it has cause to realize that many social forces outside its immediate organization must be used, if the entire community is to be christianized.

In the earliest centuries Christianity was practically limited to the life within the Church. Being surrounded by a hostile social order, and compelled to fence off its members, it created a little duplicate social order within the churches where it sought to realize the distinctively Christian social life. Its influence there was necessarily restricted mainly to individual morality, family life, and neighborly intercourse, and here it did fundamental work in raising the moral standards. On the other hand, it failed to reorganize industry, property, and the State. Even if Christians had had an intelligent social and political outlook, any interference with the Roman Empire by the low-class adherents of a forbidden religion was out of the question. When the Church was recognized and favored under Constantine and his successors, it had lost its democratic composition and spirit, and the persons who controlled it were the same sort of men who controlled the State.

The early age of the Church has had a profound influence in fixing the ideals and aims of later times. The compulsory seclusion and confinement of the age of persecution are supposed to mark the mission of the Church. As long as the social life in our country was simple and rural, the churches, when well led, were able to control the moral life of entire communities. But as social organization became complex and the solidarity of neighborhood life was left behind, the situation got beyond the institutional influence of the churches. Evidently the fighting energies of Christianity will have to make their attack on broader lines, and utilize the scientific knowledge of society, which is now for the first time at the command of religion, and the forces set free by political and social democracy. We can not restrict the modern conflict with evil to the defensive tactics of a wholly different age. Wherever organized evil opposes the advance of the Kingdom of God, there is the battle-front. Wherever there is any saving to be done, Christianity ought to be in it. The intensive economic and sociological studies of the present generation of college students are a preparation for this larger warfare with evil. These studies will receive their moral dignity and religious consecration when they are put at the service of Jesus Christ and the Kingdom of God.

SUGGESTIONS FOR THOUGHT AND DISCUSSION

I. *The Natural Drift*

1. If left alone, which way do we tend? Does a normal and sound individual need spiritual reinforcement to live a good life?

2. How do you account for the fact that the noblest movements are so easily debased?

II. *Jesus and Human Sin*

1. Did Jesus take a friendly or a gloomy view of human nature? How did the fact of sin in humanity impress him?

2. Why did he condemn so sternly those who caused the weak to stumble? Estimate the relative force of the natural weakness of human nature, and of the pressure of socialized evil, when individuals go wrong.

3. Do you agree with the exposition in the Daily Reading for the Fourth Day? Do men want to be let alone? Is this an evidence of sinful tendency?

4. What personal experiences of Jesus prompted the parable of the tares? Was the conception of Satan in Jewish religion of individual or social origin? When did it have political significance?

III. *The Irrepressible Conflict*

1. Why did Jesus foresee an inevitable conflict if the

Kingdom of God was to come? Has history borne him out?

2. Does mystical religion involve a man in conflict? Does ascetic religion? Which books him for more conflict with social evil—a life set on the Kingdom of God on earth, or a faith set on the life to come?

3. What form does the conflict with evil take in our personal life? What reinforcement does the Christian religion as a spiritual faith offer us? What personal experience have we of its failure or its effectiveness?

4. What is meant by evil being socialized? In what ways does this increase the ability of evil to defend and propagate itself?

5. What are the most dangerous forms of organized evil today? How do they work?

6. What are the most disastrous "stumbling blocks" today for working people? For business men? For students?

7. The Church sings many militant hymns. Is the Church as a whole a fighting force today?

IV. *For Special Discussion*

1. How should an individual go about it to fight concrete and socialized evils in a community?

2. How can a church get into the fight? Should the Church go into politics? Why, or why not?

3. Would Christianity be just as influential as a social power of salvation if the Christian Church did not exist?

4. Will the fight against evil ever be won? If not, is it worth fighting?

1-28-20

CHAPTER XI

THE CROSS AS A SOCIAL PRINCIPLE

Social Redemption is Wrought by Vicarious Suffering

DAILY READINGS

FIRST DAY: *The Prophetic Succession*

And he began to speak unto them in parables. A man planted a vineyard, and set a hedge about it, and digged a pit for the winepress, and built a tower, and let it out to husbandmen, and went into another country. And at the season he sent to the husbandmen a servant, that he might receive from the husbandmen of the fruits of the vineyard. And they took him, and beat him, and sent him away empty. And again he sent unto them another servant; and him they wounded in the head, and handled shamefully. And he sent another; and him they killed: and many others; beating some, and killing some. He had yet one, a beloved son: he sent him last unto them, saying, They will reverence my son. But those husbandmen said among themselves, This is the heir; come, let us kill him, and the inheritance shall be ours. And they took him, and killed him, and cast him forth out of the vineyard. What therefore will the lord of the vineyard do? he will come and destroy the husbandmen, and will give the vineyard unto others.—Mark 12: 1-9.

The vineyard parable was meant as an epitome of Jewish history. By the servants who came to summon the nation to obedience, Jesus meant the prophets. The history of the Hebrew people was marked by a unique succession of men who had experienced God, who lived in the consciousness of the Eternal, who judged the national life by the standard of divine righteousness, and who spoke to their generation as representatives of God.[1] The spirit of these men and the indirect permanent influence they gained in their nation give the Old Testament its incomparable power to impel and inspire us. They were the moving force in the spiritual progress of their nation. Yet Jesus here sketches their fate as one of suffering and rejection.

Have other nations had a succession of men corresponding to the Hebrew prophets?

Are there any in our own national history?

SECOND DAY: *The Suffering Servant of Jehovah*

Surely he hath borne our griefs, and carried our sorrows; yet we did esteem him stricken, smitten of God, and afflicted. But he was wounded for our transgressions, he was bruised for our iniquities; the chastisement of our peace was upon him; and with his stripes we are healed. All we like sheep have gone astray; we have turned every one to his own way; and Jehovah hath laid on him the iniquity of us all.

He was oppressed, yet when he was afflicted he opened not his mouth; as a lamb that is led to the slaughter, and as a sheep that before its shearers is dumb, so he opened not his mouth. By oppression and judgment he was taken away; and as for his generation, who among them considered that he was cut off out of the land of the living for the transgression of my people to whom the stroke was due?— Isaiah 53: 4-8.

---

[1] Why not give a fresh reading to the Hebrew prophets? Read them as if they had just been dug up in the East. Read them with the insight into social life developed by economic and sociological work in college. Read them with the critical social and political situations in mind. Read entire books at a sitting to absorb the spiritual valor of the prophets and their sense of God and of righteousness. George Adam Smith's "The Book of the Twelve Prophets" has fine social understanding, and gives the necessary historical background.

In the latter part of Isaiah are a number of sections describing the character and mission of "the servant of Jehovah." Whom did the writer mean? A single great personality? The suffering and exiled Hebrew nation? A godly and inspired group of prophets within the nation? The Christian Church has always seen in this servant of Jehovah a striking prophecy of Christ. The fact that the interpretation has long been in question indicates that the characteristics of the servant of Jehovah can be traced in varying degrees in the nation, in the prophetic order, in single prophets, and preeminently in the great culminating figure of all prophethood. Isaiah 53 describes the servant of Jehovah as rejected and despised, misunderstood, bearing the transgressions and chastisement of all. It is the first great formulation of the fact of vicarious suffering in humanity.

Why and how can the sins of a group fall on one?

THIRD DAY: *A Contemporary Prophet*

And as these went their way, Jesus began to say unto the multitudes concerning John, What went ye out into the wilderness to behold? a reed shaken with the wind? But what went ye out to see? a man clothed in soft raiment? Behold, they that wear soft raiment are in kings' houses. But wherefore went ye out? to see a prophet? Yea, I say unto you, and much more than a prophet. This is he, of whom it is written,

Behold, I send my messenger before thy face,
Who shall prepare thy way before thee. . . .

But whereunto shall I liken this generation? It is like unto children sitting in the marketplaces, who call unto their fellows and say, We piped unto you, and ye did not dance; we wailed, and ye did not mourn.

For John came neither eating nor drinking, and they say, He hath a demon. The Son of man came eating and drinking, and they say, Behold a glut-

tonous man and a winebibber, a friend of publicans
and sinners! And wisdom is justified by her works.
—Matt. 11: 7-10; 16-19.

To Jesus prophetism was not merely an historic fact, but
a living reality. He believed in present-day inspiration. He
and his contemporaries had seen one great prophet, fearless,
heroic, with all the marks of the type, a messenger of God
inaugurating a new era of spiritual ferment (vs. 12, 13).
But John had to bear the prophet's lot. He was then in
prison for the crime of telling a king the truth, and was
soon to die to please a vindictive woman. The people, too,
had wagged their heads over him. Like pouting children on
the public square, who "won't play," whether the game proposed is a wedding or a funeral, the people had criticized John
for being a gloomy ascetic, and found fault with Jesus for
his shocking cheerfulness. There was no way of suiting
them, and no way of making them take the call of God to
heart. Long before electricity was invented, human nature
knew all about interposing nonconductors between itself and
the truth.

*Have we ever noticed students interposing a general crit-
icism between themselves and a particular obligation?*
Can it be that one of the uses of a higher education is
to furnish greater facility in fuddling inconvenient truth?

FOURTH DAY: *Looking Forward to the Cross*

And it came to pass, when the days were well-
nigh come that he should be received up, he stedfastly set his face to go to Jerusalem.—Luke 9: 51.
In that very hour there came certain Pharisees,
saying to him, Get thee out, and go hence: for
Herod would fain kill thee. And he said unto them,
Go and say to that fox, Behold, I cast out demons
and perform cures to-day and to-morrow, and the
third day I am perfected. Nevertheless I must go
on my way to-day and to-morrow and the day fol-

lowing: for it cannot be that a prophet perish out
of Jerusalem. O Jerusalem, Jerusalem, that killeth
the prophets, and stoneth them that are sent unto
her! how often would I have gathered thy children together, even as a hen gathereth her own brood
under her wings, and ye would not!—Luke 13: 31-34.

Jesus early knew that the decision was going against him.
He saw the cross on the horizon of his life long before
others saw it. Painters have pictured him in his father's
carpenter shop, with tools on his shoulder, gazing down at
his shadow shaped like a cross. He accepted death consciously and "stedfastly set his face to go up to Jerusalem," though he knew what was awaiting him. Jerusalem
had acquired a sad preeminence as the place where the
struggles between the prophets and the heads of the nation
were settled. He saw his own death as part of the prophetic
succession. He went to it, not as a driven slave, but as a
free spirit. That jackal of a king, Herod, could not scare
him out of Galilee. His time was in his Father's hand. Today, tomorrow, and the day following, he would work, and
then he would be perfected.

FIFTH DAY: *New Prophets to Follow*

Woe unto you, scribes and Pharisees, hypocrites!
for ye build the sepulchres of the prophets, and garnish the tombs of the righteous, and say, If we had
been in the days of our fathers, we should not have
been partakers with them in the blood of the prophets. Wherefore ye witness to yourselves, that ye
are sons of them that slew the prophets. Fill ye up
then the measure of your fathers. Ye serpents, ye
offspring of vipers, how shall ye escape the judgment of hell? Therefore, behold, I send unto you
prophets, and wise men, and scribes: some of them
shall ye kill and crucify; and some of them shall ye
scourge in your synagogues, and persecute from city
to city: that upon you may come all the righteous
blood shed on the earth, from the blood of Abel the

> righteous unto the blood of Zachariah son of Bara-
> chiah, whom ye slew between the sanctuary and the
> altar. Verily I say unto you, All these things shall
> come upon this generation.—Matt. 23: 29-36.

This is the climax of the great invective against the religious leaders of the nation. The last count in the indict-
ment is that they were about to complete the record of
their fathers by rejecting and persecuting the prophets of
their generation. The fact had sunk into the public mind
that former generations had been guilty of this. "If we had
been in the days of our fathers, we should not have been
partakers with them in the blood of the prophets." Jesus
promises to make a test of this and foretells that they will
go the old way and so declare their spiritual solidarity with
the sins of the past. We see here that he thought of his
disciples as moving in the prophetic succession.

"Hast thou chosen, O my people, on whose party thou
    shalt stand,
Ere the Doom from its worn sandals shakes the dust against
    the land?"

.   .   .   .   .

"Never shows the choice momentous till the judgment hath
    passed by."

SIXTH DAY: *The Cross for All*

From that time began Jesus to show unto his disciples, that he must go unto Jerusalem, and suffer
many things of the elders and chief priests and
scribes, and be killed, and the third day be raised up.
And Peter took him, and began to rebuke him, saying, Be it far from thee, Lord: this shall never be
unto thee. But he turned, and said unto Peter, Get
thee behind me, Satan: thou art a stumbling-block
unto me: for thou mindest not the things of God,
but the things of men. Then said Jesus unto his
disciples, If any man would come after me, let him

deny himself, and take up his cross, and follow me.
For whosoever would save his life shall lose it: and
whosoever shall lose his life for my sake shall find
it.—Matt. 16: 21-25.

When the tide was turning against Jesus, he tested the
attitude of the inner circles of his disciples, and drew from
Peter on behalf of all a ringing declaration of faith and
loyalty (vs. 13-16). "From that time" Jesus began to share
with them his outlook toward death. Peter expressed the
shock which all felt and protested against the possibility.
The vehemence with which Jesus repelled Peter's suggestion
gives us a glimpse of the inner struggles in his mind, of
which we get a fuller revelation in his prayer in Gethsemane.
But instead of receding from his prediction of the cross, he
expanded it by laying the obligation of prophetic suffering
on all his disciples. Their adjustment toward that destiny
would at the same time be the settlement of their own salvation. When the Kingdom of God is at stake, a man saves
his life by losing it and loses his life by saving it, and the
loss of his higher self can not be offset by any amount of
external gain.

*Looking ahead to the profession which we expect to enter,
where do we foresee the possibility of losing our lives by
trying to save them, or of saving our lives by apparently
losing them?*

SEVENTH DAY: *The Consolations of the Prophet*

Behold, I send you forth as sheep in the midst of
wolves: be ye therefore wise as serpents, and harm-
less as doves. But beware of men: for they will
deliver you up to councils, and in their synagogues
they will scourge you; yea and before governors
and kings shall ye be brought for my sake, for a
testimony to them and to the Gentiles. But when
they deliver you up be not anxious how or what ye
shall speak: for it shall be given you in that hour

what ye shall speak. For it is not ye that speak, but the Spirit of your Father that speaketh in you. —Matt. 10: 16-20.

Jesus saith unto them, Did ye never read the scriptures,

The stone which the builders rejected,
The same was made the head of the corner;
This was from the Lord,
And it is marvellous in our eyes?—Matt. 21: 42.

Blessed are they that have been persecuted for righteousness' sake: for theirs is the kingdom of heaven. Blessed are ye when men shall reproach you, and persecute you, and say all manner of evil against you falsely, for my sake. Rejoice, and be exceeding glad: for great is your reward in heaven: for so persecuted they the prophets that were before you.—Matt. 5: 10-12.

These three passages express three great consolations for those who share prophetic opposition with Christ. They will have to face great odds; numbers and weight will be against them. But there will be a quiet voice within to prompt them and sustain them: "It is not ye that speak, but the Spirit of your Father that speaketh in you."

The second consolation is that the higher court will reverse the verdict of the lower. The stonemasons may look a stone over and conclude that it will not fit into the building; but the architect may have reserved that stone for the head of the corner. The prophet rarely lives to see his own historical vindication, but faith knows it is inevitable.

The third consolation is contained in the last of the Beatitudes. Those who are persecuted for righteousness' sake may well rejoice for the company they are in, for the Leader whose name they bear, and for the Kingdom of God which is now and ever shall be their heritage.

Imagine two classmates in the same profession, reaching the end of their career. The one has attained success, wealth, eminence, together with a reputation of never having done a courageous and self-sacrificing action, and with the consciousness that his soul has grown small as he has grown old. The other has been a fighter for the right, a conspicuous man, but has kept out of office, tasting poverty and opposition with his family, yet with the consciousness that he has had the salt of the earth for his friends and that he has put in some mighty good licks for righteousness. *Which would we rather be?*

STUDY FOR THE WEEK

Christian men have differed widely in interpreting the significance of Christ's suffering and death, but all have agreed that the cross was the effective culmination of his work and the key which unlocks the meaning of his whole life. The Church has always felt that the death of Christ was an event of eternal importance for the salvation of mankind, unique and without a parallel. It has an almost inexhaustible many-sidedness. We are examining here but one aspect. We have seen in the passages studied this week that Jesus himself linked his own suffering and rejection with the fate of the prophets who were before him and with the fate of his disciples who would come after him. He saw a red line running through history, and his own life and death were part of it. He himself generalized the social value of his peculiar experience, and taught us to see the cross as a great social principle of the Kingdom of God. He saw his death as the highest demonstration of a permanent law of human life.

I

Evil is socialized, institutionalized, and militant. The Kingdom of God and its higher laws can displace it only by conflict. "Truth forever on the scaffold, Wrong forever on the throne." This clash involves suffering. This suffering will fall most heavily on those who most completely embody the spirit and ideas of the Kingdom, and who have the necessary boldness to make the fight.

In most men the eternal moral conflict gets only con-

fused understanding. Sometimes they are aroused by senti-
mental pity or indignation, but soon tire again. If their own
interests are affected they fight well. But there are men
and women whose minds have been made so sensitive by
personal experiences or so cleansed by right education and
by the spirit of God that they take hold of the moral issues
with a really adequate understanding. Living somehow on
the outskirts of the Kingdom of Heaven, they have learned
to think and feel according to its higher ways, and when
they turn toward things as they now are, of course there is
a collision; not this time a collision of interests, but a clash
of principles, of justice with wrong, of truth with crafty
subterfuges, or of solidarity with predatory selfishness.

The life and fate of these individuals anticipates the issues
of history. This is the prophetic quality of their lives.
Working out the moral and intellectual problems in their
minds before the masses have realized them, they become the
natural leaders in the fight, clarify the minds of others, and
thus become, not only forerunners, but invaluable personal
factors in the moral progress of the race. "The single living
spirits are the effective units in shaping history; all common
tendencies working toward realization must first be con-
densed as personal forces in such minds, and then by inter-
action between them work their way to general recognition"
(Lotze). Lowell's "Present Crisis" is perhaps the most
powerful poetical expression of the prophetic function in
history.

"Count me o'er earth's chosen heroes—they were souls that
  stood alone,
While the men they agonized for hurled the contumelious
  stone,
Stood serene, and down the future saw the golden beam
  incline
To the side of perfect justice, mastered by their faith divine,
By one man's plain truth to manhood and to God's supreme design.

"By the light of burning heretics Christ's bleeding feet I
track,
Toiling up new Calvaries ever with the cross that turns
not back,
And these mounts of anguish number how each generation
learned
One new word of that grand *Credo* which in prophet-
hearts hath burned
Since the first man stood God-conquered with his face to
heaven upturned."

II

During the centuries when the Church was herself in need
of redemption and her purification was resisted by the
dominant ecclesiastical interests, such prophetic spirits as
Arnold of Brescia, Wycliffe, Huss, and Savonarola were
most frequently found battling for the freedom of the
Church from the despotic grafters inside and outside of the
hierarchy, and for the purity of the gospel. The Church was
a chief part of the social order, and the reform of the Church
was the preeminent social problem. Today the Church is
on the whole free from graft, and as openminded as the
state of public intelligence permits it to be. Therefore the
prophet minds are now set free to fight for the freedom of
the people in political government and for the substitution
of cooperation for predatory methods in industry, and the
clash is most felt on that field.

The law of prophetic suffering holds true as much as
ever. Probably no group of men have ever undertaken to
cleanse a city of profit-making vice without being made to
suffer for it. In the last thirty years this country has watched
eminent men in public life in various great cities making a
sincere drive to break the grip of a grafting police machine,
or of a political clique, or of public service corporations. For
a while such a man has public sentiment with him, for all
communities have a desire to be moral. But when it becomes
clear that he really means what he says, and that important

incomes will be hurt, powerful forces set on him with abuse and ridicule, try to wreck his business or health, and side-track his political ambitions. An eminent editor in the Middle West, speaking before the Press Association of his State several years ago, said: "There is not a man in the United States today who has tried honestly to do anything to change the fundamental conditions that make for poverty, disease, vice, and crime in our great cities, in our courts and in our legislatures, who, at the very time at which his efforts seemed most likely to succeed, has not been suddenly turned upon and rent by the great newspaper publications." A volume of truthful biographical sketches of such leaders would give us a history of the cross in politics, and would tell us more about Christianity as an effective force in our country than some church statistics.

III

Jesus took the sin of throttling the prophets very seriously. It is sin on a higher level than the side-stepping of frail human nature, or the wrongs done in private grievances. Since the Kingdom of God is the highest thing there is, an attempt to block it or ruin it is the worst sin. Our hope for the advance of the race and its escape from its permanent evils is conditioned on keeping our moral perceptions clear and strong. Suffocating the best specimens of moral intelligence and intimidating the rest by their fate quenches the guiding light of mankind. Is anything worse?

Jesus held that the rejection of the prophets might involve the whole nation in guilt and doom. How does the action of Caiaphas and a handful of other men involve all the rest? By virtue of human solidarity. One sins and all suffer, because all are bound together. A dominant group acts for all, and drags all into disaster. This points to the moral importance of good government. If exploiters and oppressors are in control of society, its collective actions will be guided and determined by the very men who have most to fear from the Kingdom of God and most inclination to stifle the prophetic voices.

But the same solidarity which acts as a conductor of sin will also serve as a basis to make the attack of the righteous few effective for all. If the suffering of good men puts a just issue where all can see and understand, it intensifies and consolidates the right feeling of the community. The suffering of a leader calls out passionate sympathy and loyalty, sometimes in a dangerous degree. In the labor movement almost any fault is forgiven to a man who has been in prison for the cause of labor, and death for a popular cause will idealize the memory of very ordinary or questionable characters. But if the character of a leader is pure, suffering accredits him and gives him power. The cross had an incomparable value in putting the cause of Christianity before the world. It placed Jesus where mankind could never forget him, and it lit up the whole problem of sin and redemption with the fire of the greatest of all tragedies.

> "The cross, bold type of shame to homage turned,
>   Of an unfinished life that sways the world."

IV

But not all righteous suffering is socially effective. A good man may be suppressed before he has won a following, or even before he has wrought out his message in his own mind, and his suppression leaves only a few bubbles on the waters of oblivion. In that case his life has failed to discharge the redemptive force contained in it. It only adds a little more to the horror and tragedy of a sinful, deaf, and bloodstained world. Many of the men whose lives ebbed away behind the cruel silence of the walls of the Spanish Inquisition, were such men as Spain needed most. What saving effect did their death exercise? The uncounted patriots whose chains have clanked on the march to Siberian exile, have not yet freed Russia from its blind oligarchy. Our faith is that their lives were dear to God, and that their sorrows and the bitter tears of those who loved them are somehow part of an accumulating force which will one day save Russia. But this is religious faith, "a conviction of things not seen." We can not prove it. We can only trust.

Meanwhile it is our business to see that no innocent blood is wasted. Pain is a merciful and redemptive institution of nature when pain acts as an alarm-bell to direct intelligent attention to the cause of the pain. If pain does not force the elimination of its own cause, it is an added evil. The death of the innocent, through oppression, child labor, dirt diseases, or airless tenements, ought to arrest the attention of the community and put the social cause of their death in the limelight. In that case they have died a vicarious death which helps to redeem the rest from a social evil, and anyone who utilizes their suffering for that end, shows his reverence for their death. We owe that duty in even higher measure to the prophets, who are not passive and unconscious victims, but who set themselves intelligently in opposition to evil. The moral soundness of a nation can be measured by the swiftness and accuracy with which it understands its prophetic voices, or personalities, or events. The next best thing to being a prophet is to interpret a prophet. This is one of the proper functions of trained and idealistic minds, such as college men and women should possess. The more the Kingdom of God is present, the less will prophets be allowed to suffer. When it is fully come, the cross will disappear.

V

The social principle of the cross contains a challenge to all who are conscious of qualities of leadership. Let the average man do average duties, but let the strong man shoulder the heavy pack. It is no more than fair that persons of great natural power should deliberately choose work involving social hardships. At present the theory seems to be that the strong have a right to secure places where they will be freed from the necessity of exerting themselves, and can lay their support on the shoulders of the poor. That is the law of the cross reversed. Our semi-pagan society has always practiced vicarious suffering by letting the poor bear the burdens of the rich in addition to their own. Instead of encouraging the capable to hunt after predatory profit and entrusting public powers to those who have been most successful in preying, we ought to encourage solidaristic feeling, and give both power and honor to those who are ready to serve the commonwealth at severe cost to themselves.

What has the principle of the cross to say to college men and women? If they have an exceptional outfit, let them do exceptional work. A knight in armor was expected to charge where others could not venture. A college education entitles a Christian man to some hard knocks. It seems contemptible for us to walk off with the pleasures and powers of intellectual training, and to leave the work of protecting children and working girls against exploitation to men and women without education, without leisure, and without social standing, who will have to pay double the tale of effort for every bit of success they win. In some European countries foreign mission service has been left mainly to men and women of the artisan class. In our country college men and women have volunteered for it. That is as it ought to be. On the other hand, in the struggle for political liberty the European universities have taken a braver and more sacrificial part than has ever fallen to our lot.

Those who are conscious of a prophetic mission have a redoubled motive for a clean, sober, and sincere life. Especially in its initial stages an ethical movement is identified with its leaders and tested by their character. A good man can get a hearing for an unpopular cause by the trust he inspires. His cause banks on his credit. The flawed private character or dubious history of a leader is a drag. It is worse yet if a man whose name has long been a guarantee for his message, backslides and brings doubt upon all his previous professions. Cases could be mentioned where noble movements were wrecked for years because a leader forfeited his honor. Constant fighting against evil involves subtle temptations. To stand alone, to set your own conviction against the majority, to challenge what is supposed to be final, to disregard the conventional standards—this may lead to dangerous habits of mind. If we propose to spread a lot of canvas in a high wind, we need the more ballast in the hold. Through the thin partitions of a summer hotel, a man heard Moody praying God to save him from Moody. Imagine what it must be to lose standing and honor among your fellow men by secret weakness. Imagine also the poignant pain if your disgrace pulls down a cause which you have loved for years and which in purer days you vowed to follow to its coronation.

SUGGESTIONS FOR THOUGHT AND DISCUSSION

I. *Vicarious Suffering and Social Progress*

1. Does suffering benefit humanity? Titus crucified thousands of Jews during the destruction of Jerusalem. Did their death have any saving effect?
2. What is the connection between vicarious suffering and social salvation?

II. *Prophetic Suffering*

1. What was the fate of the Old Testament prophets? What was their influence in the life of Israel? To what extent is Mark 12:1-9 a fair epitome of the treatment of the prophets by the Hebrew nation?
2. What is the significance of Isa. 53:4-8? Why and how can the sins of a group fall on another?
3. Where did Jesus see the continuity of prophetic suffering in his own times?
4. What place did he give to vicarious suffering in the life of his followers and in the conquest of the Kingdom? How does the law of the Cross connect with the fact of solidarity?

5. In what respects was Christ's Cross unique? In what respects does it express a general spiritual law?

III. *Vicarious Suffering Today*

1. Give instances of persons in public life today whose careers were wrecked because they assailed socialized evil or graft. How does this differ from the fate of the prophets?

2. Are the sacrifices of prophetic leaders ever useless and actually ineffective? Do you feel an inward protest against that? On what ground?

3. To what extent is the call to be a Christian a challenge to vicarious suffering? What social significance, then, would Christian baptism have?

4. Is there anything wrong with a Christian life which does not incur suffering?

5. Would suffering be normal in the religious life of the young?

6. Why does this social principle apply especially to college men and women?

IV. *For Special Discussion*

1. What qualities constitute a man a prophet?

2. Are there embryonic prophets? Or spent prophets? Is a prophet necessarily a saint?

3. Do prophets arise where religion deals with private life only? What is the social value of prophetic personalities?

4. Name men in secular history and literature who have the marks of the prophet. Any in recent times?

5. Does learning create prophetic vision or blur it?

6. Does the ordinary religion today put a man in line for the Cross or for a job as a bank director?

7. Can you think of anything that would bring the Cross back into the life of the churches today?

8. Would vicarious suffering diminish if society became Christianized?

CHAPTER XII

A REVIEW AND A CHALLENGE

The Social Principles of Jesus Demand Personal Allegiance and Social Action

DAILY READINGS

FIRST DAY: *The Social Mission of Christians*

Ye are the salt of the earth. . . . Ye are the light of the world.—Matt. 5: 13, 14.

"Jesus speaks here with the consciousness of an historic mission to the whole of humanity. Yet it was a Nazarene carpenter speaking to a group of Galilean peasants and fishermen. Under the circumstances, and at the time, it was an utterance of the most daring faith—faith in himself, faith in them, faith in what he was putting into them, faith in faith. Jesus failed and was crucified, first his body by his enemies, and then his spirit by the men who bore his name. But that failure was so amazing a success that today it takes an effort on our part to realize that it required any faith on his part to inaugurate the Kingdom of God and to send out his apostolate." [1]

If the antiseptic and enlightening influence of the sincere followers of Jesus were eliminated from our American communities, what would be the presumable social effects?

SECOND DAY: *The Great Initiator of the Kingdom of God*

At that season Jesus answered and said, I thank thee, O Father, Lord of heaven and earth, that thou

[1] "Christianity and the Social Crisis," p. 415.

didst hide these things from the wise and understanding, and didst reveal them unto babes: yea, Father, for so it was well-pleasing in thy sight. All things have been delivered unto me of my Father: and no one knoweth the Son, save the Father; neither doth any know the Father, save the Son, and he to whomsoever the Son willeth to reveal him. Come unto me, all ye that labor and are heavy laden, and I will give you rest. Take my yoke upon you, and learn of me; for I am meek and lowly in heart: and ye shall find rest unto your souls. For my yoke is easy, and my burden is light. —Matt. 11: 25-30.

This is one of the most thrilling passages in the Bible. It has always been understood as a call to intimate religion, as the appeal of a personal Saviour to those who are loaded with sin and weary of worldliness. But in fact it expresses the sense of a revolutionary mission to society.

Jesus had the consciousness of a unique relation to the Father, which made him the mediator of a new understanding of God and of life (v. 27). This new insight was making a new intellectual alignment, leaving the philosophers and scholars as they were, and fertilizing the minds of simple people (v. 25). It is an historical fact that the brilliant body of intellectuals of the first and second centuries was blind to what proved to be the most fruitful and influential movement of all times, and it was left to slaves and working men to transmit it and save it from suppression at the cost of their lives.

Then Jesus turns to the toiling and heavy laden people about him with the offer of a new kind of leadership—none of the brutal self-assertion of the Cæsars and of all conquerors here, but a gentle and humble spirit, and an obedience which was pleasure and brought release to the soul.

These words express his consciousness of being different, and of bearing within him the beginnings of a new spiritual constitution of humanity.

When individuals have really come under the new law of Christ, does Jesus make good?

Would he also make good if humanity based its collective life on the social principles which we have studied?

If the choice is between Cæsar and Christ, which shall it be?

THIRD DAY: *The Kingdom of Truth*

Pilate therefore entered again into the Prætorium, and called Jesus, and said unto him, Art thou the King of the Jews? Jesus answered, Sayest thou this of thyself, or did others tell it thee concerning me? Pilate answered, Am I a Jew? Thine own nation and the chief priests delivered thee unto me: what hast thou done? Jesus answered, My kingdom is not of this world: if my kingdom were of this world, then would my servants fight, that I should not be delivered to the Jews: but now is my kingdom not from hence. Pilate therefore said unto him, Art thou a king then? Jesus answered, Thou sayest that I am a king. To this end have I been born, and to this end am I come into the world, that I should bear witness unto the truth. Every one that is of the truth heareth my voice. Pilate saith unto him, What is truth?

And when he had said this, he went out again unto the Jews, and saith unto them, I find no crime in him.—John 18: 33-38.

All kingdoms rest on force; formerly on swords and bayonets, now on big guns. To overthrow them you must prepare more force, bigger guns. Jesus was accused before Pilate of being leader of a force revolution aiming to make him king. He claimed the kingship, but repudiated the force. To his mind the absence of force resistance was characteristic of his whole undertaking. Instead, his power was based on the appeal and attractiveness of truth. When Pilate heard "truth" he thought he had a sophist before him, one more builder of metaphysical systems, and expressed the skepticism of the man on the street: "What is truth?" But Jesus was not a teacher of abstract doctrine, whatever his expounders have made of him. His mind was bent on realities. If we substitute "reality" for "truth" in his saying here, we shall get near his thought.

Which is more durable, power based on force, or power based on spiritual coherence?

FOURTH DAY: *A Mental Transformation*

> I beseech you therefore, brethren, by the mercies of God, to present your bodies a living sacrifice, holy, acceptable to God, which is your spiritual service. And be not fashioned according to this world: but be ye transformed by the renewing of your mind, that ye may prove what is the good and acceptable and perfect will of God.—Rom. 12: 1, 2.

In the first century the Christians were a new social group, confronting the social order of the Roman Empire with a new religious faith, a revolutionary hope, and a powerful impulse of fraternity. Those who had come out of pagan society still felt the pull of its loose pleasures and moral maxims, and of its idolatry. Paul here challenges them to submit fully to the social assimilation of the new group. It involved an intellectual renewal, a new spiritual orientation, which must have been searching and painful. It involved the loss of many social pleasures, of business profit and civic honor, and it might at any time mean banishment, torture, and death. The altar symbol of sacrifice might become a scarlet reality. Yet see with what triumphant joy and assurance Paul speaks.

If a student should dedicate himself to the creation of a Christian social order today, would it still require an intellectual renewing?

Would it cramp him or enlarge him?

FIFTH DAY: *The Distinctive Contribution of Christ*

> There was the true light, even the light which

lighteth every man, coming into the world. He was in the world, and the world was made through him, and the world knew him not. He came unto his own, and they that were his own received him not. But as many as received him, to them gave he the right to become children of God, even to them that believe on his name: who were born, not of blood, nor of the will of the flesh, nor of the will of man, but of God. And the Word became flesh, and dwelt among us (and we beheld his glory, glory as of the only begotten from the Father), full of grace and truth. For the law was given through Moses; grace and truth came through Jesus Christ.—John 1: 9-14, 17.

Here is the tragedy of the Gospel story, seen from a long perspective and stated in terms of Greek philosophy. The Light which lighteth every man, the *Logos* through whom God had created the *kòsmos,* had come to this world in human form, and been rejected. But some had received him, and these had received a new life through him, which made them children of God. They had discovered in him a new kind of spiritual splendor, characterized by "grace and truth." Even Moses had contributed only law to humanity; Christ was identified with grace and truth.

How would you paraphrase the statements of John to express the attitude of nineteen centuries to Christ?

What has he in fact done for those who have received him?

What would be the modern equivalent of "grace and truth" to express the distinctive contribution of Christ to human history?

SIXTH DAY: *The Master of the Greatest Game*

Therefore let us also, seeing we are compassed about with so great a cloud of witnesses, lay aside every weight, and the sin which doth so easily beset us, and let us run with patience the race that is set before us, looking unto Jesus the author and perfecter of our faith, who for the joy that was set before him endured the cross, despising shame, and hath sat down at the right hand of the throne of God. For consider him that hath endured such gainsaying of sinners against himself, that ye wax not weary, fainting in your souls.—Heb. 12: 1-3.

The man who wrote the little treatise from which this is quoted saw the history of humanity summed up in the live spirits who had the power of projection into the future. Faith is the quality of mind which sees things before they are visible, which acts on ideals before they are realities, and which feels the distant city of God to be more dear, substantial, and attractive than the edible and profitable present. Read Hebrews 11. So he calls on Christians to take up the same manner of life, and compares them with men running a race in an amphitheatre packed with all the generations of the past who are watching them make their record. But he bids them keep their eye on Jesus who starts them at the line and will meet them at the goal, and who has set the pace for good and fleet men for all time.

What is the social and evolutionary value of the men of "faith" in the sense of Hebrews 11?

Have we left Jesus behind us by this time?

SEVENTH DAY: *The Beginning of the Greatest Movement in History*

Now after John was delivered up, Jesus came into Galilee, preaching the gospel of God, and saying, The time is fulfilled, and the kingdom of God is at hand: repent ye, and believe in the gospel.

And passing along by the sea of Galilee, he saw Simon and Andrew the brother of Simon casting a net in the sea; for they were fishers. And Jesus said unto them, Come ye after me, and I will make you to become fishers of men. And straightway they left the nets, and followed him. And going on a little further, he saw James the son of Zebedee, and

John his brother, who also were in the boat mending
the nets. And straightway he called them: and they
left their father Zebedee in the boat with the hired
servants, and went after him.—Mark 1 : 14-20.

Here we have the beginning of organized Christianity.
This is the germinal cell of that vast social movement of
which foreign missions, the establishment of the American
Republic, and the modern labor movement are products. It
began with repentance, faith, and self-sacrificing action, and
it will always have to advance by the same means. To those
four men Jesus was an incarnate challenge. He dared them
to come, and promised to put their lives on a higher level.
He stands over against us with the same challenge. He
points to the blackened fields of battle, to the economic injustice and exploitation of industry, to the paganism and
sexualism of our life. Is this old order of things to go on
forever? Will our children, and their children, still be
ground through the hopper? Or have we faith to adventure
our life in a new order, the Kingdom of God?

STUDY FOR THE WEEK

Has our study of the "Social Principles of Jesus" revealed
a clear and consistent scheme of life, worthy of our respect?

I

We have seen that three convictions were axiomatic with
Jesus, so that all his reasoning and his moral imperatives
were based on them, just as all thought and work in physics
is based on gravitation. These convictions were the sacredness of life and personality, the solidarity of the human
family, and the obligation of the strong to stand up for
all whose life is impaired or whose place within humanity is
denied.

It can not be questioned that these convictions were a
tremendous and spontaneous force in the spirit of Jesus.
That alone suffices to align him with all idealistic minds,

to whom man is more than matter, more than labor force, a mysterious participant of the spiritual powers of the universe. It aligns him with all men of solidaristic conviction, who are working for genuine community life in village and city, for a nation with fraternal institutions and fraternal national consciousness, and for a coming family of nations and races. It aligns him with all exponents of the democratic social spirit of our day, who feel the wrongs of the common people and are trying to make the world juster and more fraternal.

The best forces of modern life are converging along these lines. There is no contradiction between them and the spirit of Jesus. On the contrary, they are largely the product of his spirit, diffused and organized in the Western world. He was the initiator; we are the interpreters and agents. Nor has he been outstripped like an early inventor and discoverer whose crude work is honored only because others were able to improve on it. Quite the contrary; the more vividly these spiritual convictions glow in the heart of any man, the more will he feel that Jesus is still ahead, still the inspiring force. As soon as we get beyond theory to life and action, we know that we are dependent for the spiritual powers in modern life on the continued influence of Jesus Christ over the lives of others.

II

We saw in the second place that Jesus had a social ideal, the Reign of God on earth, in which God's will would be done. This ideal with him was not a Utopian and academic fancy, but the great prize and task of life toward which he launched all his energies. He called men to turn away from the evil ways of the old order, and to get a mind fit for the new. He set the able individuals to work, and put the spirit of intense labor and devotion into them. He proposed to effect the transition from the old order to the new by expanding the area of moral obligation and raising the standards of moral relationships.

By having such a social ideal at all, he draws away from all who are stationary and anchored in the world as it is; from all who locate the possibility of growth and progress in the individual only; and from all whose desire for perfection runs away from this world to a world beyond the grave.

By moving toward the new social order of the Kingdom of God with such wholeness of determination, he is the constant rebuke for all of us who are trying to live with a "divided allegiance," straddling between the iniquities of force, profit, and inhumanity, and the fraternal righteousness of the Gospel we profess to believe. Jesus at least was no time-server, no Mr. Facing-both-ways, no hypocrite; and whenever we touch his elbow by inadvertence, a shiver of reality and self-contempt runs through us.

III

We saw in the third place that Jesus dealt with serious intelligence with the great human instincts that go wrong.

The capacity for leadership and the desire for it have fastened the damning institutions of tyranny and oppression on humanity and tied us up so completely that the rare historical chances of freedom and progress have been like a tumultuous and brief escape. Yet Jesus saw that ambition was not to be suppressed, but to be yoked to the service of society. In the past, society was allowed to advance and prosper only if this advanced the prosperity and security of its ruling classes. Jesus proposed that this be reversed, so that the leaders would have to earn power and honor by advancing the welfare of society by distinguished service at cost to themselves.

The desire for private property has been the chief outlet for selfish impulses antagonistic to public welfare. To gain private wealth men have slaughtered the forests, contaminated the rivers, drained the fertility of the soil, monopolized the mineral wealth of the country, enslaved childhood, double-yoked motherhood, exhausted manhood, hog-tied community undertakings, and generally acted as the dog in the manger toward humanity. Jesus opposed accumulation without moral purpose, the inhumanity of property differences, and the fatal absorption of money-making. Yet he was not ascetic. It is probably safe to say that he would not be against private property in so far as it serves the common good, and not against public property at all.

Like ambition and the property instinct, the religious impulse may go wrong, and subject society to its distortions or tyranny. Jesus always stood for an ethical and social outcome of religion. He sought to harness the great power of religion to righteousness and love. With a mind so purely religious we might expect that he would make all earthly and social interests subservient to personal religion. The fact that he reversed it, seems clear proof that he was socially minded and that the Kingdom of God as a right social organism was the really vital thing to him.

IV

We have seen, finally, that Jesus had a deep sense of the sin and evil in the world. Human nature is frail; men of evil will are powerful; organized evil is in practical control. Consequently social regeneration involves not only growth but conflict. The way to the Kingdom of God always has been and always will be a *via dolorosa*. The cross is not accidental, but is a law of social progress.

These conceptions together seem to shape up into a consistent conception of social life. It is not the modern scientific scheme, but a religious view of life. But it blends incomparably better with modern science than the scholastic philosophy or theology of an age far nearer to us than Jesus. It is strange how little modern knowledge has to discount in the teachings of Jesus. As Romanes once pointed out,[2] Plato followed Socrates and lived amidst a blaze of genius never since equalled; he is the greatest representative of

[2] G. J. Romanes, "Thoughts on Religion," p. 157.

human reason in the direction of spirituality unaided by revelation; "but the errors in the dialogues reach to absurdity in reason and to sayings shocking to the moral sense."

The writer of this little book has come back to an intensive study of Jesus at intervals of years, and every time it was like a fresh revelation, leaving a sense of mental exhilaration and a new sense of joy in truth. Never was there a feeling that Jesus was exhausted and had nothing more to say.

For a true valuation of his intellectual contribution to mankind we must remember that we have not a page of his own writing. We are dependent on the verbal memory of his disciples; so far as we know, nothing was written down for years. The fragments which survived probably had to stand the ordeal of translation from the Aramaic to the Greek. Simply from the point of view of literature, it is an amazing thing that anything characteristic in Jesus survived at all. But it did. His sayings have the sparkle of genius and personality; the illustrations and epigrams which he threw off in fertile profusion are still clinchers; even his humor plays around them. Critics undertake to fix on the genuine sayings by internal evidence. Only a mind of transcendent originality could win its way to posterity through such obstructions.

But we ought not to forget the brevity of our material when we try to build up a coherent conception of his outlook on society. There is little use in stickling on details. The main thing is the personality of Jesus, his religious and ethical insight into the nature and needs of the social life of mankind, the vital power of religious conviction which he was able to put behind righteousness, and the historical force which he set going through history.

From the indirect influences which Jesus Christ set in motion, no man or woman or child in America can escape. We live on him. Even those who attack the Christian Church, or who repudiate what they suppose Christ to stand for, do so with spiritual weapons which they have borrowed from him. But it does make a great difference whether the young men and women of our day give their conscious and intelligent allegiance to Christianity or hold aloof in mis-understanding. Without them the Christian movement will mark time on old issues. With them it will dig new irriga-tion channels and string the wires for new power trans-mission.

In return, Christianity can do more for students than they themselves are likely to realize in youth. Men grow tired. Their moral enthusiasm flags. Scientific sociology may remain academic, cold, and ineffective. We need in-spiration, impulse, will power, and nothing can furnish such steady accessions of moral energy as living religion. Science and the Christian faith combined are strong. Those who succeed in effecting a combination of these two without insincerity or cowardice are the coming leaders.

If a student's mind has given inward consent to the teach-ings of Jesus in this course of study, that constitutes an appeal for personal discipleship. Can we go with Christ in living out these principles, and meanwhile draw on his spirit-ual wealth to build up our growing life? If there is a student who can not at present affirm all that the Christian Church holds concerning the nature of Christ, why should he not approach him as the earliest disciples did, by personal love and obedience, following him and cooperating with him in the business of the Kingdom of God, and arriving in time at full faith in his Messiahship? A great and firm faith is the product and prize of a lifetime of prayer and loving action. "Light is sown to the righteous." As we gather the wisdom of life, and find that while we move from knowledge to knowledge, we are also advancing from mystery to mystery, many of us will be ready and glad to join in the highest affirmation of faith about Jesus Christ, in whom we have learned to see God.

> "If Jesus Christ is a man,
>   And only a man, I say
> That of all mankind I cleave to him,
>   And to him I cleave alway.

"If Jesus Christ is a God,
And the only God, I swear
I will follow him through heaven and hell,
The earth, the sea, and the air."
—RICHARD WATSON GILDER.

If Christianity henceforth is to discharge its full energy in the regeneration of social life, it especially needs the allegiance of college men and women who have learned to understand to some degree the facts and laws of human society. The development of what is called "Social Christianity" or "the social gospel," is a fusion between the new understanding created by the social sciences, and the teachings and moral ideals of Christianity. This combination was inevitable; it has already registered social effects of the highest importance; if it can win the active minds of the present generation of college students, it will swing a part of the enormous organized forces of the Christian Church to bear on the social tasks of our American communities, and that will help to create the nobler America which we see by faith.

Christians have never fully understood Christianity. A purer comprehension of its tremendous contents is always necessary. Think what it would signify to a local community if all sincere Christian people in it should interpret their obligation in the social terms which we have been using; if they should seek not only their own salvation, but the reign of God in their own town; if they should cultivate the habit of seeing a divine sacredness in every personality, should assist in creating the economic foundations for fraternal solidarity, and if, as Christians, they should champion the weak in their own community. We need a power of renewal in our American communities that will carry us across the coming social transition, and social Christianity can supply it by directing the plastic force of the old faith of our fathers to the new social tasks.

Jesus was the initiator of the Kingdom of God. It is a real thing, now in operation. It is within us, and among us, gaining ground in our intellectual life and in our social institutions. It overlaps and interpenetrates all existing organizations, raising them to a higher level when they are good, resisting them when they are evil, quietly revolutionizing the old social order and changing it into the new. It suffers terrible reverses; we are in the midst of one now; but after a time it may become apparent that a master hand has turned the situation and laid the basis of victory on the wrecks of defeat. The Kingdom of God is always coming; you can never lay your hand on it and say, "It is here." But such fragmentary realizations of it as we have, alone make life worth living. The memories which are still sweet and dear when the fire begins to die in the ashes, are the memories of days when we lived fully in the Kingdom of Heaven, toiling for it, suffering for it, and feeling the stirring of the godlike and eternal life within us. The most humiliating and crushing realization is that we have betrayed our heavenly Fatherland and sold out for thirty pieces of silver. We often mistake it. We think we see its banner in the distance, when it is only the bloody flag of the old order. But a man learns. He comes to know whether he is in God's country, especially if he sees the great Leader near him.

SUGGESTIONS FOR THOUGHT AND DISCUSSION

I. *The Social Principles of Jesus*

1. Sum up the social principles of Jesus which we have worked out in this course.

2. Do they seem incisive? Would they demand far-reaching social changes? What changes?

3. What conceptions acquired in philosophical and social science studies connect fruitfully with the principles of Jesus? Do any scientific conceptions conflict with the essential ideas of Jesus?

II. *Social Salvation*

1. What is your frank estimate of the value of the social

principles of Jesus as a religious and ethical basis for the regeneration of society?

2. Does the spiritual development of modern life tend toward the position of Jesus or away from it?

3. What opportunities and methods does modern life offer for carrying out these principles in our social order?

4. If society cannot be saved under the spiritual leadership of Jesus, how can it be saved?

III. *The Leader*

1. As this course proceeded, has our respect or reverence for Jesus Christ increased or diminished? In what ways?

2. Would it be possible to join the forward Christian forces in working for the Kingdom of God even if the theological questions are still unsolved in our minds?

3. What seem now the best methods of carrying out these principles in our own community and in the world?

IV. *For Special Discussion*

1. Does the salvation of society seem to make the salvation of the individual unnecessary or trivial? Have you lost interest in it?

2. How should social and personal salvation connect?

3. What would a loyal religious dedication to Christ and Christianity mean to our scientific social intelligence?

4. What would it mean to the course of our life?